D1572495

EMIGRANTS
FROM IRELAND
TO AMERICA,
1735-1743

A Transcription of the Report of the
Irish House of Commons into
Enforced Emigration to America

By Frances McDonnell

Copyright © 1992
Genealogical Publishing Co., Inc.
1001 N. Calvert Street
Baltimore, Maryland 21202
All Rights Reserved
Library of Congress Catalogue Card Number 91-77067
International Standard Book Number 0-8063-1331-5
Made in the United States of America

Introduction

uring the seventeenth and eighteenth centuries over 60,000 men, women and children were involuntarily transported from the British Isles to the American colonies. The vast majority of these people were felons, but there were a number of political and religious dissidents such as the Cromwellian transportees of the 1650s. The English courts were far more likely to order the transportation of prisoners than were the Scottish or Irish courts, banishing about 50,000 prisoners to the colonies to work as indentured servants. The Scottish authorities ordered fewer than 3,000 prisoners to be transported and the Irish courts approximately 4,000.

In 1719 an Act was introduced into the Irish House of Commons for "the better and more effectual apprehending and transporting of felons and others," and given Royal assent on 8 March 1725.

The kidnapping and shipment of children to America and their sale as indentured servants began to cause concern, and in January 1743 the Irish Government established a committee to examine the whole system of transportation in detail.

Information presented to the committee contains valuable data pertaining to 2,000 Irish men and women transported to the American colonies during the mid-eighteenth century. As a result of this committee's investigations, further legislation was introduced in the Irish House of Commons in January 1752 tightening up the rules governing the transportation of prisoners.

The following is a transcript of the Report of the committee, as contained in the *Journal of the House of Commons of the Kingdom of Ireland,* Vol. 7 (1796).

Frances McDonnell
September 1991

Report of the Irish House of Commons
into Enforced Emigration to America

Journal of the House of Commons
of the Kingdom of Ireland,
Volume 7, 1796

Mr Archibald reported from the Committee, appointed to re-consider the several returns of the felons and vagabonds, ordered for transportation these seven years last past, and to inquire how many persons were actually transported, how many died or escaped before transportation, how much money hath been raised for those purposes, and to whom paid, the matter, as it appeared to them, with the resolutions of the Committee thereupon; and he read the report in his place, and afterwards delivered the same in at the table, where the report was again read; and the resolutions were read a second time, and agreed unto by the House, and the report and resolutions are as follows.

The Speaker,
The Committee appointed to inspect and examine the several returns made to the House of the felons and vagabonds ordered for transportation these seven years last past, and to inquire how many persons were actually transported, how many died or escaped before transportation, how much money hath been raised for those purposes, and to whom paid, have met (according to order) and re-considered the report made to the House the seventh instant, and it having appeared to the Committee during the progress of this examination, that several frauds and abuses had been committed and carried on by Sub Sheriffs and other persons in the execution of the laws now inforce in this kingdom for transporting convicts felons and vagabonds; and it likewise appearing to the Committee, that the execution of those laws hath been most notoriously neglected, the Committee directed me (for the better information of the House) to report the facts as they appeared to them specially, with the resolutions of the Committee thereupon, and the same are as follow.

The Committee, on inspection of the several lists of convict felons and vagabonds, thought proper to draw up a general abstract thereout, distinguishing the number of such persons and the sums raised for their transportation, likewise distinguishing the several provinces in this kingdom, and the counties in each province respectively. The Committee also apprehending it necessary for their better information to call before them the several persons following.

Mr Henry Gonne, Town-clerk of Dublin, being examined, produced two books to the Committee, wherein the names not only of all convict felons and vagabonds ordered for transportation, but also the names of other persons who enter into indentures with merchants transporters to be transported to his Majesty's plantations, and the term of years for which they bind themselves respectively, and that have been bound by indentures before the Lord Mayors of the City of Dublin for these seven years last past; and transport such felons, made answer, he had not any such bonds or recognizances in his office; but that if any such bonds or recognizances were to be found, they were in the keeping or power of the several Clerks attending the Lord Mayors of Dublin for their respective years; being asked if any certificates were returned by any of the merchants transporters to his office of their having transported such felons and vagabonds, made answer, there were not any such returned to his office; the Committee thereupon ordered the Clerk attending the Lord Mayor of Dublin to attend the Committee.

Mr Edward Scriven attending in the absence of Mr Lewis Jones, Clerk to the present Lord Mayor (and now sick) who informed the Committee, that there were not any bonds or recognizances of merchants transporters in the Lord Mayor`s Clerk`s office taken by former Lord Mayors, but that he believed each Lord Mayor or his Clerk kept those bonds themselves: that there were two bonds taken by the present Lord Mayor of Dublin of merchants transporters which he produced to the Committee, the condition of which bonds, as the Committee conceived, were not agreeable to the requisites in the Act of Parliament, which obliged the merchant to return a certifice in eighteen months of such felons being transported.

The Committee, for their better information, thought proper also to call before them several merchants of Dublin who have heretofore transported numbers of such felons and vagabonds, and perticularly Mr Joseph Wild merchant, being examined, laid before the Committee an account in writing of the names of all convict felons and vagabonds by him and company transported for these seven years last past, with the names of the ships and the places in America to which they were bound, and said that he and company received about three pound a man for their transportation, except ten of them who were transmitted from the Counties of Kilkenny, Kerry and Corke, and they only got from the Sub-sheriffs or other officers that delivered them over, forty shillings a man, although he believes five or six pounds a man was presented and paid by the Counties respectively.

Mr John Hornby, merchant, being examined before the Committee, laid before them an account of the convict felons and vagabonds by him transported, with no account of the money by him received, and informed the Committee that the chief magistrates of Dublin never demanded of him any certificate of such persons being transported.

Mr Thomas Cooke of Dublin, merchant, being examined, laid before the Committee an account of what felons and vagabonds he had transported, with an account of what money he had received for those purposes; Mr Cooke also laid before the Committee a bill of sale from America of a considerable number of such persons being effectually transported, which was very satisfactory to the Committee.

Mr John Langley, merchant, of Dublin, being examined, laid before the Committee an account of what convict felons and vagabonds he had transported these seven years last past, with an account of the names of the ships they were put on board, the several Counties from whence they were transmitted, and the money by him received from the several high and Sub-sheriffs and gaolers of the said Counties respectively; being further examined, informed the Committee, that the most he ever got for transporting any of the said convicts was three pounds a man, and for others of them but two pounds ten shillings, (although he is credibly informed and believes there were presented on the several Counties respectively five or six pounds a man): Mr Langley also produced to the Committee a certificate from the naval office in America of his having transported seventy-three persons convict felons and vagabonds; he further said, that he had given bonds of fifty pounds penalty for the transportation of each of said felons and vagabonds before the Lord Mayor of Dublin, but does not apprehend that there is any part of the condition of such bonds or recognizances that require he should return a certificate in eighteen months of their being transported, for that he was never called on by any such chief magistrate for any such certificate.

Mr Redmond Kane late Sub-sheriff of the County of Dublin, being examined before the Committee, laid before them a list of convict felons and vagabonds by him contracted for with merchants for their transportation, to the number of thirty-five, and the sums of money by him received, amounting to one hundred and seventy-five pounds: being further examined, said he had five pounds for each convict felon, but confessed he only paid to the merchant transporter about three pounds a man for some, and near four pounds a man for others of them.

Marks Synnott, Esq; late High-sheriff of the County of Dublin, being examined before the Committee, laid before them, a list of convict felons and vagabonds, for which money was presented to be paid to him off said County, and being further examined said, that there was five pounds a man presented to be paid to him, but that he only paid the merchants transporters two pounds then shillings a man.

Mr Richard Rickison, present Sub-sheriff of the County of Dublin, was called upon and examined, who laid before the Committee a list of the convict felons and vagabonds by him contracted for to be transported, with an account of the money by him received for those purposes; and being examined touching the money so presented, said he had paid all the money so presented to the merchants transporters for such transportation, except the last sum in said list, which was not as yet raised.

Your Committee, in obedience to the order of the House, requiring them to inform the House how many of such convict felons and vagabonds had died in goal or made their escape before transportation, called before the Committee the Coroners of the City of Dublin, who being examined, made a return of a list of felons and vagabonds who died in Newgate these seven years last past upon whose bodies inquests were held; and the Committee having examined Mr Thomas Smith, keeper of Newgate in the City of Dublin, ordered him to lay before them a list of such persons as died in Newgate and upon whom inquests were held these seven years last past, and Mr Smith laid a list before the Committee accordingly, and upon comparing the returns made by the Coroners, and the said return by Mr Smith, your Committee find there is a variation or difference between said lists of eighteen names left in Mr Smith`s return than in the Coroners return, and Mr Smith being examined touching such variation, could not give your Committee any other satisfaction or information, than that he had made a return of such names as he had in his books.

The Committee further crave leave to observe, that in the courts of their examination, they found it necessary to order the treasurers of the county of Dublin, and County of the City of Dublin, to lay before the Committee an account of all money presented in the said counties respectively, and ordered to be paid to any High-sheriff or Sub-sheriff, or other persons for these seven years last past, not only for the transportation of convict felons and vagabonds, but also for what other particular service, sums of money were presented and paid to such Sheriffs or Under-sheriffs, which said returns were accordingly made to he Committee, and are as follow.

Mr Alexander Carroll, treasurer for money raised by presentments in the County of the City of Dublin, laid before the Committee an account of all money presented to be paid for transporting felons and vagabonds from said City for these seven years last past, amounting to one thousand one hundred and sixty one pounds, with the names of the merchants transporters who received the same.

Mr John King, treasurer for the County of Dublin, being called before the Committee, laid before them three several papers or accounts, the first,

No I
An account of what money raised in the King`s bench on the county of Dublin, for the transportation of felons and vagabonds for these seven years last past.

No II

An account of what money raised at the Quarter-sessions for the County of Dublin, for these seven years past, for transporting felons and vagabonds.

No III

An account of all sums of money that have been presented in the said County of Dublin, and paid to High or Sub-sheriffs for these seven years last past, and for what particular service, over and above what particular sums were presented to be paid them for transporting felons and vagabonds.

The Committee beg leave to observe, on reading this last account of the treasurer for the County of Dublin, No III, whereby the sum of four hundred and ninety seven pounds two shillings and six pence is set forth to be presented and raised off the inhabitants of the County of Dublin, and paid to the several Sub-sheriffs in the said return mentioned, for particular services, that of the said sum of four hundred and ninety seven pounds two shillings and six pence, there has fore these seven years last past, only the sum of sixty pounds been presented and allowed of, and raised by the grand juries impannelled at his Majesty's court of King's-Bench, and that the remaining sum of four hundred and thirty-seven pounds two shillings and six pence has been raised by presentments, allowed of at the several Quarter-sessions held at Kilmainbam for the said County, for the purposes in the said account mentioned, which sum of four hundred and thirty seven pounds two shillings and six pence, so levied on the inhabitants of said County, your Committee humbly apprehend is no way warranted by law, and the same being of a very extraordinary nature, the Committee did not think proper to come to any particular resolution therein, but humbly submit the same to the consideration of the House.

The Committee proceeded further, to call before them Mr John Cooke late Sub-sheriff of the County of Dublin, and now Marshall of the marshalsea of the City of Dublin, who by order of the Committee laid before them, and account of what money he received by presentment of the grand juries of the county of Dublin, in the year 1739, at the four Quarter-sessions held at Kilmainham in the County of Dublin, and in Trinity and Hillary terms in the said year, by presentment of the grand juries at said terms in his Majesty's court of King's-Bench, amounting in the whole to the sum of one hundred and twenty pounds, the which return, and the services for which the said sums are represented to have been presented and paid, are likewise humbly submitted to the consideration of the House.

No 1

A General abstract of the number of convict felons and vagabonds mentioned in the lists returned, who were ordered for transportation of this kingdom for these seven years last past, together with an acc of what sums of money have been raised for those purposes.

<u>Province of Leinster</u>

	No	L	s	d
Kings's-Bench, City of Dublin	161	268	00	00
County of the City of Dublin	304	1152	00	00
County of Dublin	50	262	00	00
County of Lowth	29	96	12	11
County of the town of Drogheda	17	40	00	00
County of Meath	44	325	2	9
County of Kildare	31	148	00	00
King's County	18	127	16	00
Queen's County	38	267	10	1
County of Catherlagh	33	192	00	00
County of Kilkenny	48	182	00	00
County of the City of Kilkenny	16	96	00	00
County of Wexford	45	182	17	5
County of Wicklow	31	191	00	00
County of Westmeath	60	270	00	00
County of Longford	12	70	00	00
	937	3870	19	2

<u>Province of Munster</u>

	No	L	s	d
County of Corke	133	566	00	00
County of the City of Corke	125	406	05	00
County of Limerick	60	338	01	11
County of the City of Limerick	12	61	00	00
County of Kerry	68	413	10	04
County of Tipperary	89	301	04	06
County of Waterford	41	193	00	00
County of the City of Waterford	14	53	00	00
	542	2332	01	09

6

Province of Ulster

	No	L	s	d
County of Monaghan	37	204	00	0
County of Armagh	28	129	00	00
County of Antrim	50	250	00	00
County of Downe	42	200	00	00
County of Cavan	28	113	00	00
County of Fermanagh	17	110	00	00
County of Tyrone	26	156	00	00
County of Donegal	25	240	00	00
City and County of Londonderry	43	161	00	00
County of the town of Carrickfergus				
	296	1563	00	00

Province of Connaught

	No	L	s	d
County of Galway	43	206	00	00
County of the town of Galway	2	10	00	00
County of Leitrim	18	68	00	00
County of Mayo	9	45	00	00
County of Rosscommon	25	75	00	00
County of Sligoe	18	122	00	00
County of Clare	30	138	00	00
Total convict felons	145	662	04	0

A list of the several convict felons and vagabonds who have been ordered for transportation from his Majesty's court of King's-bench, and the several commissions of Oyer and Terminer held for the County of the City of Dublin, from the twenty-third day of February one thousand seven hundred and thirty-five, to the twenty-fifth day of October one thousand seven hundred and forth-three, inclusive.

Stephen Nowlan
John Richardson
William Hughes
Bryan Keegan
Mary Creighton als Dillon
Ellinor Keally
James Quin

George Medlicot
Dennis Moran
Edward Moran
Bridget Connor
Peter Quinn
Rose Divininy
Mary Maguire

Arthur Murphy
Francis Flood
Magaret Tornbury
Martin Bourke
Timothy Flanigan
John Campbell
Patrick Connor
John Savage
Patrick Bryan
Laughlin Murphy
Peter Cannon
Ann Costelloe
William Whelan
Thmas Kelly
Andrew Graham
Michael Morris
Matthew Connelly
James Knight
Mary Walsh
James Connor
James Maguire
William Erwin
James Walsh
Bryan Farrell
Robert Bryan
John Clark
Margaret Shepherd or Isbetto
Peter Sweetman

Tobias Cavanagh
Bryan Devin
Richard Begg
Matthew Spencer
Barthol. McManus
James McCowly
Dennis Dunn
James Carney
Philip Fitzsimons
James Walsh
Patrick Reilly
Alice Carney
Joseph Norton
Mary Byrne
Patrick Molloy
Charles Rourke
Richard Tyrrell
Alice Collins
Andrew Cleary
Mary Bently
Edmond Hacket
William Dowling
Ellinor Hussey
Roger Dougherty
Roger Sweeny
Robert Cussack
Henry White

I humbly certifie the above list, to be a true list of the several persons who were ordered for transportation as fellons and vagabonds, tried and presented at his Majesty's court of King's-bench, and at the several commissions of the Oyer and Terminer held for the City of Dublin, from the twenty-third day of February one thousand seven hundred and thirty-five to the twenty-fifth day of October one thousand seven hundred and forty three inclusive; and I further certifie that there has not been any sum or sums of money presented or raised by the several grand juries at the commissions of Oyer and Terminer, have never presented any sums of money for any use whatsoever, not having power to do so.   Date this twenty-ninth day of November, 1743.

St. John Bowden, Dep Clerk Crown

A list of the several convicts felons and vagabonds who have been ordered for transportation from his Majesty's court of King's-bench, and the several commissions of Oyer and Terminer held for the County of Dublin from the twenty-third day of February one thousand seven hundred and thirty-five, to the twenty-fifth day of October one thousand seven hundred and forty-three, inclusive.

James Moore
In Easter term 1738, the grand jury of the County of Dublin presented the sum of twelve pounds to be paid to William Scriven Sub-Sheriff of said County, for transporting the above James Moore and one James Cullen whom I do not find to be either tried or presented at the King's-bench on Commissions.

Michael Donoghoe   Patrick Flynn
Robert Hart   Laughlin Cox
Martin Smith   John Benn

In Michalmas term 1738, the grand jury of said County presented the sum of thirty-six pounds to be paid the said William Scriven, for transporting the above persons.

Philip Magennis   Patrick Dowling
John Reillyn   Mary Lawless
Patrick Dowling   Hugh Glascoe

In Hillary term 1739, the grand jury of said County presented the sum of thirty pounds to be paid Mr John Cooke, then Sub-sheriff of said County for transporting the above persons.

William Murphy   John Hill
Edmund Graham   John Gogarty
John Redmond   Bryan McAtire
James Walsh   Thomas Hoy
John Dorman   Francis Neal

In Trinity term 1741, the grand jury of the said County pesented the sum of fifty pounds to be paid Mr Redmond Kean, then Sub-sheriff of said County for transporting the said William Murphy, and said other persons.

Mary Maguire	Mary Lawler
John Howard	Edward Wilson
Willian Shortly	Catherine Delany
Owen Murphy	Thomas Rider
Hugh Reilly	Mary Colligan

In Michaelmas term 1741, the grand jury of said County presented the sum of fifty pounds to be paid to the said Redmond Kean for transporting the above persons.

Peter Reilly	Terress Dignam
Elizabeth Hyland	Thomas Kearnan
Patrick Killkelly	Patrick Johnston
Matthew Ternan	Sarah Bryan
Rachel Evisston	John Carroll
Walter Hughes	John Ferrell

In Hillary term 1741, the grand jury of said County presented the sum of seventy-five pounds to be paid said Redmond Kean, for transporting the above persons, together with John Gogarty, for whole transportation, money was presented in Trinity term 1741, and for William Kane and George Forrester, who I do not find have been ordered to be transported either at the term of commission.

Daniel Dolan	Patrick Byrn
James Delany	

In Trinity Term 1743, the grand jury of said County presented the sum of fifteen pounds to be paid to Mr Richard Rickison present Sub-sheriff of said County, for transporting the above persons.

Barbara Jones	Ann Connolly
William Banning	David Anderson
John Moor	Henry Keating

Ann Jones	William Carr
Mary Dowling	Joan Ennis
Mary Hobbs	Darby Hanton
Mary Butterfield	Edward Cawlan
John Conway	Patrick Bath
Thomas Connaughty	Bridget Maley
Thomas Tallent	Catherine Wall
William Tyrell	James Laughlin
John Reilly	Mary Gorman
Arthur McMahon	Patrick Carroll
Thomas Ptolemy	John Neal
Daniel Fox	Bridget Dolan
Patrick Cempsey	Thomas Cantillon
Daniel Guiraty	Faughny Farrell
Thady Grey	Robert Brady
Mary Congrave	Thomas Cahill
Ralph Venebles	Malachi Bergin
Dudley Byrne	Graham Bradford
John Farrell	James Fitzpatrick

I humbly certify the foregoing list to be a true list of the several persons who were ordered to be transported as felons and vagabonds, tried and presented at his Majesty's court of King's-bench, and at the several commissions of Oyer and Terminer held for the county of Dublin, from the twenty-third day of February one thousand seven hundred and thirty-five, to the twenty fifth day of October, one thousand seven hundred and forty-three, incl five, and that the several grand juries of said county, at the several terms aforesaid, presented the several sums of money herein before mentioned, for the transportation of the several persons for which said money is mentioned to be raised and paid, amounting in the whole to the sum of two hundred and forty-eight pounds, and I do not find that there was any other sum or sums of money presented by the several grand juries of said County, for the transportation of any of the other persons in this list contained during said time.   Dated this twenty-ninth day of November 1743.

St. John Bowden, Dep Clerk Crown

A list of all the persons who have been tried and convicted at the several general Quarter-sessions of the peace held for the County of the City of Dublin, and ordered to be transported for these seven years last past; as also of all those who have been presented and transported as vagabonds during the said time, with an account of what money has been presented and raised for the aforesaid purposes, the said list commencing midsummer Sessions 1736, and ending midsummer Sessions 1743.

Midsummer Sessions 1736

Judith Lester
Mary Bryan
Henry Curtis
Robert Withers
George Atkinson

Jane Appleby
Jane Gaffney
William Burke
Patrick Reilly

Michaelmas Sessions 1736

Ellenor Prendergast
Andrew Warren
John Sheridan

John Fergusson
John Ball

Christmas Sessions 1736

James McDonough
Thomas Farrell
Cornelius Watkins
Honora Gorman/Cossee
James Malone
John Mercy
Mary Jocob

Walter Farrell
Catherine Ryan/Carpenter
John Davis
Walter Sceale
Martha Donnelly
Catherine Malone
Barnaby Higgins

Easter Sessions 1737

Mary Carroll
Mary Morgan
James Flood

Mary Kelly
Judith Gorman
Archibald Vickers

Midsummer Sessions 1737

Mary Neill
Catherine Martin
Mary Morris
William McCormick
John Sherry

Mary/Catherine Deering
John Raw
John Whelan
John Terrill
Darby Heany

Michaelmas Sessions 1737

Richard Kelly
Mary Shea
Robert Harding
Mary Keenan
John Ponsonby
Ann Carthy

Catherine Kennedy
Mary Norton
John Callaghan
John Long
Rose Dogherty

Christmas Sessions 1737

Bryan Ferrell
John Williams
William Sharp
Thomas Butterton

Thomas Roe
Sarah Keely
James Kernes

Easter Sessions 1738

Sarah Dungan
Constance McDaniell

Mary Ryan/Fitzgerald
John Quinlan

Midsummer Sessions 1738

Mary Christian
Mary Kelly
Patrick Long
Neil Dogherty
Patrick Garvey

Dorothy Ryan
James Rourk
Ellenor Kelly
Mary Mealy
James Murray

Michaelmas Sessions 1738

James Clynch
Thomas McAnally
John Bryan
Andrew Isaac
Mary Waters

William Mills
Hugh Brady
Thomas Wright
Jane Melchan
John Smith

Christmas Sessions 1738

Thomas Carroll
Philip Corbet
Bryan Fitzsimons
Ennis Quinn
Mary Buyer
Patrick Mullan

Edward Murphy
Catherine Butler
Ann Owens
James Field
Richard Bryan
Edward Mullan

Easter Sessions 1739

Patrick Darling
Patrick McKendrick
Thomas Sullivan

Mary Ponsonby
Elizabeth Stephens
Mary Byrne

Midsummer Sessions 1739

John Gilstrap
Patrick Finn
George Kane
Hugh Morris
John Tobin

Andrew Owens
Dennis Gill
Elizabeth Winsmore
Laurence Bellow

Michaelmas Sessions 1739

Thomas Scanlon
Thomas Reagan
Mary Murphy

Thomas Curtis
Martha Kelly

Christmas Sessions 1739

Miles Bryan
James Coghlan
John Mulvey
Patrick Mathews
Robert Murphy
Thomas Connor
Mary Clancy

Thomas Murphy
John Carney
Margaret Kelly
James Fernsly
Robert Handy
Patrick Devin

14

Easter Sessions 1740

John Enderson
James Lord
Matthew Murphy
John Mullowney
Daniel Clayton

John Brien
Michael Morgan
Elizabeth Nangle
John Carney

Midsummer Sessions 1740

Rose Mealy
Catherine Reilly
Patrick Caulan
Lucy Coleman

Judith Lamb
Christopher Hickey
Elizabeth Mooney/Long
Walter Sheeban

Michaelmas Sessions 1740

James Donovan
Ann Bray
Henry Brien
John Lawler
James McDaniell
Thomas Patterson

Peter Coghlan
Ann Nugent
Thomas Elmes
John Bourke
Patrick Duffy

Christmas Sessions 1740

Thomas Finn
Mary Halfpenny
Catherine Conolly
Henry Coffee
William Carney
George Reeny
John Caffry
Ann Hanly
Elizabeth Mercy
Mary Heany

Matthew Maher
Elizabeth Russell
Richard Terrill
Philip Downey
Honora McNally
Arthur O'Neile
Margaret Donovan
Elizabeth Camaran
Mary Joyce
John Smith

Easter Sessions 1741

James Connor
Penelope Gorman
Jane Kelly
Thomas Wilkinson
Ann Lacy
Daniel Nowland/Richard English

Thomas King
John Callaghan
Judy Keiffe
Pidgeon Finlay
Margaret Keiffe

Midsummer Sessions 1741

Barthol. Glavin
James Williams
John Brown

John Dowling
Edward Staunton

Michaelmas Sessions 1741

Elinor Sandford
Mary Ryan
Ellenor Joyce
John Patterson
Patrick Kelly
Peter Hopper
Laurence Chambers
Henry Fitzsimmons

John O'Donnell
Jane Ryan
Elizabeth Browne
Margaret Conolly
Thomas Dowling
Mary Hussey
Patrick Carroll

Christmas Sessions 1741

Richard Keon
Margaret Glasco
Patrick Cooley
Ann Barnes
Mary Smith
Daniel Brady
Bridget Clark
Mason Donnelly
James Doran
Christopher Smith
Mary Heydon
Alice Tresso

Edmund Fitzgerald
John Conford
Mary Casheen
William Dempsey
William Carty
Hugh Redmond
William Neal
Catherine Doyle
Susanna Bourke
Jane Ball
Mary Roche

Easter Sessions 1742

John Jones
Nicholas Furlong
Catherine Johnston

James Newman
Margaret Johnston

Midsummer Sessions 1742

Mary Hutchison
Ellenor Hutchinson
Mary Maguire
Ann Keary
Judith Brady
John Maugher
Ann Malone
Daniel Sheaghan
Dorothy Lord
James Lynagh
Thomas Rooney
Elizabeth Redford
Catherine Reilly
Ann Taylor
Mary Fitzgerald

James Quin
Margaret Hand
Mary Martin
Patrick Marpenter
John Bannor
James Russell
Owen Mulhollan
Elizabeth Smith
John Lynch
Mary Stones
John Rooney
Sarah Goodwin
William Butler
Bulking Juggy
Magaret Mcdonnell

Michaelmas Sessions 1742

Mary Farrell
Thomas Burk
Daniel Whealan
Mary Long
Mary Heany

Mary Fitzsimmons
John Walsh
William Hogan
Thomas Healy

Christmas Sessions 1742

Tobias Butler
Michael Doyle
Mary Jones

Richard Condron
Alice McDaniell
Thomasin Lock

Easter Sessions 1743

Catherine Norris
Elizabeth Haverty
Bridget White
John Masterson

Peter Mullan
Catherine Carroll
Michael Ludlow

Midsummer Sessions 1743

Winifred Linford
Mary Byrne
Dominick Hogan
Edward Dogherty/Hot Eye
Margaret Dillon

Catherine Byrne
Laurence Langan
Patrick Smith
William Kennedy
Mary Drury

I humbly certifie that the foregoing is a true list of all the convict felons
and vagabonds who have been ordered at the several Quarter-sessions of
the peace, held for the County of the City of Dublin, to be transported for
these seven years last past, and that the exact sum of three pounds
sterling has been presented by the several grand juries for the County of
the said City for each person transported, and that the several sums
presented to be raised on the inhabitants of the said City of Dublin within
the time aforesaid, for transporting felons and vagabonds, including those
convicted at the several commissions of Oyer and Terminer held for the
said City of Dublin, and at the aforesaid Sessions of the peace, amount in
the whole to the sum of one thousand one hundred and fifty-two pounds
sterling, dated the twenty-fifth day of November 1743.

Henry Gonne, Clerk Peace County City of Dublin

Abstract of presentments for money at the several Quarter sessions of the
County of the City of Dublin, commencing Midsummer Sessions 1737, and
ending Midsummer Sessions 1743, delivered at the bar by Mr Henry Gonne,
Sabbati 26 die Novembris, 1743, and ordered to lie upon the table.

Midsummer Sessions 1737

A presentment for sixty-three pounds to James Stevenson, Esq, for
transporting twenty-one convicts persuant to the statute.

Michaelmas, 1737

The like for one hundred and two pounds to Mr Isaac Kelsick merchant, for transporting thirty-four felons and vagabonds persuant to the statute.

Christmas, 1737

The like for seventy-five pounds to Mr John Martin for transporting twenty-five felons and vagabonds as aforesaid.

Same Sessions

The like for twenty-one pounds to Mr Joseph Weld merchant, for transporting seven felons as aforesaid.

Easter Sessions 1738 (in one presentment)

The like for three pounds to Thomas Robinson for transporting a convict, six pounds to William Tissen for transporting two convicts, twelve pounds to Peter Cullen for transporting four convicts, and fifteen pounds to Alexander Montgomery for transporting five convicts.

Michaelmas, 1738

A presentment for six pounds to Richard Durham for transporting two felons as aforesaid.

Midsummer, 1739

The like for one hundred and eleven pounds to Mr Joseph Weld merchant, for transporting thirty-seven felons and vagabonds as aforesaid, and three pounds to Mr Samuel Horner, merchant, for transorting one felon as aforesaid.

The like for thirty-three pounds to Mr Isaac Kelsick, merchant, for transporting eleven felons and vagabonds as aforesaid.

The like for thirty-nine pounds to Mr John Hornby, merchant, for transporting thirteen felons and vagabonds as aforesaid.

Midsummer, 1740

The like for forty-five pounds to Mr Joseph Weld, merchant, for transporting fifteen felons and vagabonds as aforesaid.

The like for sixty pounds to Mr Samuel Lyons, merchant, for transporting twenty felons and vagabonds as aforesaid.

The like for fifteen pounds to Mr Thomas Steel, merchant, for transporting five felons and vagabonds as aforesaid.

Christmas, 1740

The like for sixty-three pounds to Mr Thomas Cooke, merchant, for transporting twenty-one felons and vagabonds as aforesaid.

Midsummer, 1741

A presentment for twenty-seven pounds to Walter Codd, for transporting nine felons and vagabonds pursuant to the statute.

The like for twenty-seven pounds to Jacob Willard for transporting nine felons and vagabonds as aforesaid.

The like for sixty-nine pounds to Mr Samuel Lyons and Oliver Bird for transporting twenty-three felons and vagabonds as aforesaid.

Christmas, 1741

The like for ninety pounds to Mr Joseph Weld, merchant, for transporting thirty felons and vagabonds as aforesaid.

The like for fifty-four pounds to Mr Richard Goodman, merchant, for transporting eighteen felons and vagabonds as aforesaid.

Midsummer, 1742

The like for ninety-six pounds to Mr John Langley, merchant, for transporting thirty-two felons and vagabonds as aforesaid.

Michaelmas, 1742

The like for forty-eight pounds to Mr James Campbell, merchant, for transporting sixteen felons and vagabonds as aforesaid.

Easter, 1743

The like for forty-eight pounds to Mr John Martin for transporting sixteen felons and vagabonds as aforesaid.

Midsummer, 1743

The like for twenty-one pounds to Mr John Langley, merchant, for transporting seven felons and vagabonds as aforesaid.

I humbly certify that the foregoing is an exact abstract of all the presentments made by the grand-juries at the several Sessions held for the county of the City of Dublin, commencing midsummer Sessions, 1737, to this Time, for transporting felons and vagabonds pursuant to the statute.   Dated this twenty-fifth day of November, 1743.

Henry Gonne, Clerk Peace County City Dublin

A list of all convict felons and vagabonds who have been ordered for transportation at the general Quarter-sessions of the peace, held for the county of Dublin, for these seven years last past.

SESSIONS

January 1741
    John McGwire
    Hester McGwire
    Jane McGwire

April, 1742
   Thomas Murphy
   Catherine Byrne
   Judith Freeman/Byrne
   Mary Anderson

October, 1742
   David Lawler
   William Flin/Leathercap

January, 1742
   Thomas Moran

October, 1743
   Patrick Purcel
   Joan Barefoot

Thomas Green, Dep Clerk Peace for the County of Dublin

A list of all convicted felons and vagabonds who have been ordered for transportation for seven years last past in the several Counties of Meath, County of the town of Drogheda, and County of Lowth in the North East circuit of Ulster and provice of Leinster.

COUNTY OF MEATH

Assizes Dates	Persons Ordered for Transportation	Crimes	Money presented for that purpose		
			L	s	d
22 Mar 1736/7					
25 Jul 1737			4 0	0 0	0 0
10 Apr 1738	Michael Kelly	Grand larceny)			
	Patrick Smyth	Like)	2 6	0 0	0 0
24 Jul 1738	Honorah Kennedy	Vagabond	1 8	0 0	0 0
22 Mar 1738	Patrick Moran	Grand Larceny			
	Michael Cavenagh	Grand Larceny			
7 Sep 1739			1 2	0 0	0 0
16 Apr 1740	Thomas Magauran	Vagabond			
	John Kelly	Like			
	Mary Byrne	Petty Larceny			
6 Aug 1740	Owen Byrne	Vagabond)			
	Christopher Dowd	Like)	1 8	0 0	0 0
Cont'd					

Assizes dates	Persons ordered for transportation	Crimes	Money presented for that purpose		
			L	s	d
8 Apr 1741	James McCabe	Like			
	James Carroll	Grand Larceny			
	Thomas Carroll	Like			
	Mathew Mooney	Vagabond			
	Owen Meenagh	Like			
	James Daly	Grand Larceny			
	Robert Ball	Like			
	Francis Kelly	Vagabond			
	Patrick McMahon	Forging a bond			
8 Jul 1741	Bryan McCabe	Vagabond)			
	Matthew Dudley	Petty Larceny)			
	John Canlon	Vagabond)			
	John Connor	Like)	91	00	00
	John Bannon	Grand Larceny			
28 Apr 1742	James Caulan	Like)			
	George Smyth	Vagabond)			
	Henry Shaffrey	Grand Larceny)			
	Richard Swords	Like)			
	Daniel Garvin	Petty Larceny)			
	James Rogers	Grand Larceny)			
	Thomas Russell	Like)			
	Michael Cunningham	Like)			
	Owen McGuire	Vagabond)			
	Patrick Meehan	Grand Larceny)			
	Patrick Macken	Like)	24	00	00
26 Jul 1742	Patrick Heyland	Vagabond			
	Thomas Williams	Petty Larceny			
	Patrick McBryan	Like			
11 Apr 1743	Nicholas Hamill	Grand Larceny)			
	Bridget Reilly	Vagabond)			
	Matthew Murtagh	Grand Larceny)			
	Patrick Bray	Vagabond)	96	00	00
18 Aug 1743	Henry Finnegan	Grand Larceny)			
	Richard Murphy	Vagabond			
			335	00	00

COUNTY OF THE TOWN OF DROGHEDA

Assizes Dates	Persons ordered for transportation	Crimes	Money presented for that purpose		
			L	s	d
19 Apr 1737	James Berrill	Grand Larceny			
	Catherine Caffry	Like	10	00	00
18 Aug 1737					
13 Mar 1737					
28 Jul 1738	Patrick Reilly	Grand Larceny)			
	Dominick Flynn	Vagabond)			
20 Apr 1739	Thomas Boden	Like)			
13 Aug 1739	Patrick Kelly	Like)			
20 Mar 1739	Michael Tyrrell	Like)			
11 Aug 1740	William Morgan	Like)	10	00	00
	John Rafferty	Grand Larceny	15	00	00
13 Jul 1741					
29 Mar 1742	Dennis Lynagh	Like	6	00	00
	Michael McCullagh	Vagabond			
	Andrew Tallon	Grand Larceny			
30 Jul 1742	Edward Clinton	Vagabond			
	John Carton younger	Like			
16 Mar 1742					
5 Aug 1743	Thomas Hern	Grand Larceny			
	James Fitz-Symons	Vagabond	_____		
			40	00	00

COUNTY LOWTH

Assizes Dates	Persons ordered for transportation	Crimes	Money presented for that purpose		
			L	s	d
20 Apr 1737			4	3	00
10 Aug 1737	Mary Reilly	Vagabond			
	James Mathews	Like)			
	Ever Mathews	Like)	15	4	6
14 Mar 1737 Cont'd	Owen Boyle	Like			

24

Assizes Dates	Persons ordered for transportation	Crimes	Money presented for that purpose		
			L	s	d
29 Jul 1738	Bryan Downey	Petty Larceny			
	Edward McCullam	Vagabond			
	Robert Phillips	Like			
17 Apr 1739	John McDonnell	Like			
	Arthur McGarrety	Like			
14 Aug 1739	James McCabe	Like			
21 Mar 1739	Margaret Johnston	Grand Larceny)			
	Patrick Fedigan	Vagabond)			
	Patrick Mohan	Grand Larceny)	20	00	00
12 Aug 1740	Owen Callaghan	Vagabond	0	15	00
12 Mar 1740	James Murphy	Like			
	James McArdle	Like			
14 Jul 1741	James Gallagher	Like)			
	Hugh White	Like)			
	William Hill	Grand Larceny)	10	00	00
30 Mar 1742	Patrick Carragher	Like			
	Patrick English	Vagabond)			
2 Aug 1742	John Bray	Like)			
	Patrick Sharkey	Like)			
	Francis Ohear	Like)			
	James Stewart	Like			
	Edward Riccard	Like)	15	00	00
17 Mar 1742			17	5	5
6 Aug 1743	John McGowran	Vagabond			
	Ellenor Daly	Grand Larceny			
	Thomas Roe Cawlan	Vagabond	_____		
			96	12	11

I do hereby certifie that in the foregoing sheets are contained a list of all convict felons and vagabonds who have been ordered for transportation for these seven years last past, as also the several sums of money presented for those purposes in the several Counties of Meath, County of the town of Drogheda, and County of Lowth, in the North-East circuit of Ulster and province of Leinster.   Dated this nineteenth day of November, 1743,

Thomas Kanning deputy Clerk of the Crown

25

COUNTY OF KILDARE

A list of all convicted felons and vagabonds who have been ordered for transportation for seven years last past in the several Counties of Kildare, King's County, Queen's County, County of Carlow, County of Kilkenny, County of the City of Kilkenny, County of Wexford, and County of Wicklow in the province of Leinster.

Assizes Dates	Persons ordered for transportation	Crimes	Money presented for that purpose		
			L	s	d
21 Mar 1736-37	Abraham Murphy	Vagabond)			
	John Mechan	Like)			
	Phelim Murphy	Like)	22	00	00
5 Aug 1737	Mary Murphy	Like	6	00	00
5 Aug 1737	Thomas Byrn	Like)			
	Owen Dunn	Like)	12	00	00
31 Jul 1738	John Finnegan	Vagabond			
11 Apr 1739					
6 Aug 1739	John Doyle	Like˜			
	John Vardin	Like			
	Simon Delahunty	Like			
	James Kelly	Petty Larceny			
17 Mar 1739					
2 Aug 1740	James Quin	Vagabond)			
	David Hardin	Like)	18	0	0
9 Mar 1740	Thomas Potts	Vagabond			
	John Cavanagh	Grand Larceny			
	Edward Roe	Vagabond			
15 Aug 1741	Patrick Mulholland	Grand Larceny)			
	Neal Daly	Like)	36	0	0
29 Mar 1742					
28 Aug 1742	Mary Byrn	Vagabond)			
	Owen Slaffery	Like)			
	Edward Dowdall	Like)			
	Patrick Kinshella	Like)	24	0	0

Cont'd

26

Assizes Dates	Persons ordered for transportation	Crimes	Money presented for that purpose		
			L	s	d
14 Mar 1742	Michael Malone	Vagabond			
	George Fishburn	Grand Larceny)			
	Thomas Bourk	Like)			
	Sarah Ryan	Like)			
	Mary Bourk	Like)			
	Richard Morres	Like)			
	Catherine Muckleroy	Like)			
	James Neal	Like)			
	Theobald Bourk	Like)	30	0	0
4 Aug 1743			108	0	0

KING'S COUNTY

Assizes Dates	Persons ordered for transportation	Crimes	Money presented for that purpose		
			L	s	d
25 Mar 1737	John Frain	Vagabond)			
	John Careless	Like)			
	Patrick Moran	Like)	19	16	0
15 Aug 1737	James Rourk	Like			
14 Mar 1737	James Rourk	Grand Larceny)			
	John McDaniell	Vagabond)			
	Barthol. Cormack	Grand Larceny)	6	0	0
7 Aug 1738					
7 Apr 1739	Thady Mahon	Like)	30	0	0
	William Fitzgerald	Like)	12	0	0
30 Jul 1739	John Connor	Vagabond			
	Owen Crow	Grand Larceny			
21 Mar 1739			6	0	0

Cont'd

Assizes Dates	Persons ordered for transportation	Crimes	L	s	d
5 Aug 1740					
13 Mar 1740	John Quin	Like)			
7 Aug 1741	Thomas McDaniell	Like)			
	Alexander McDaniel	Like)			
	Laughlin Lynan	Like)	18	0	0
2 Apr 1742					
25 Aug 1742	Nicholas Mihin	Grand Larceny)			
	Thomas Goodale	Vagabond)	12	0	0
28 Mar 1742			18	0	0
27 Jul 1743	Lawrence Hand	Grand Larceny	6	0	0
			127	16	0

QUEEN'S COUNTY

Assizes Dates	Persons ordered for transportation	Crimes	L	s	d
29 Mar 1737					
10 Aug 1737	Patrick Cushan	Grand Larceny			
17 Mar 1737	William Kelly	Like			
3 Aug 1738	James Cantwell	Vagabond)			
	John Fitzgerald	Like)	20	0	0
2 Apr 1739	Catherine Connor	Like)			
	William Ellord	Perjury)			
	Andrew Morrin	Grand Larceny)			
	Grizel Delany	Like)	20	0	0
2 Aug 1739	John Lawler	Vagabond)			
	Daniel Kelly	Grand Larceny)			
	Mary Foran	Like)	40	0	0
25 Mar 1740	Charles Delany	Like	18	0	0
6 Aug 1740	John Long	Vagabond	12	0	0
7 Nov 1740 Com.	Henry Neal	Grand Larceny			
of Oyer & Term.	Philip Fitzgerald	Like			
17 Mar 1740	Patrick Grandy	Like			
	Thomas Horahan	Like			

Cont'd

Assizes Dates	Persons ordered for transportation	Crimes	Money presented for that purpose		
			L	s	d
4 Aug 1741	James Bourke	Vagabond			
	Thomas Lynham	Grand Larceny			
	Paul Dunn	Like			
	Michael Donohoe	Like			
6 Apr 1742	Bryan Connor	Vagabond)			
	Darby Kelly	Grand Larceny)			
	Patrick King	Like)	75	0	0
21 Aug 1742	John Conran				
	William Doogan				
	Patrick Grace				
	Michael Hogan				
	Roger Carney) *	These and the			
	William Delany) *	foregoing four all			
	Thomas Goodwin) *	convicted of felony			
	John Sherlock) *	of death but pardoned by the government for transportation.	56	0	0
22 Mar 1742	Patrick Moore	Grand Larceny			
	Roger Gormill	Vagabond			
	Joan Butler	Grand Larceny			
	Dennis Ryan	Like			
30 Jul 1743	Thady Champion	Like)			
	Edmond Conrahy	Vagabond)	26	0	0
			267	0	0

COUNTY OF CARLOW

Assizes Dates	Persons ordered for transportation	Crimes	Money presented for that purpose		
			L	s	d
4 Apr 1737					
2 Aug 1737	Bryan Donald	Vagabond			
	Dennis Brennan	Like	12	0	0
23 Mar 1737	Daniel Bourk	Like			
27 Jul 1738					
29 Mar 1739			6	0	0
9 Aug 1739	Michael Corran	Like			
	James Corran	Like			
	Patrick Synnott	Like			
	Thomas Reddy	Like			
	Edm. Reddy	Like			
29 Mar 1740	Edm. McCabe	Like			
30 Jul 1740	Roger Farrell	Like)			
	John Brack	Like)			
	Thomas Brack	Like)	18	0	0
23 Mar 1740	Thady Clark	Like			
11 Aug 1740	Charles Toole	Like)			
	Mich. Martin	Like)			
	James Doyle	Like)			
	Matth. Purcell	Like)			
	Miles King	Like)			
10 Apr 1742	Anne Hoey	Like)			
	John Nowlan	Like)	6	0	0
	Bryan Doran	Like	42	0	0
	Dennis Doyle	Like			
	James Walsh	Like	24	0	0
	John Kealy	Like			
	Will. Lynchy	Like			
	Edm. McEvary	Like			
26 Apr 1742	Peter Fitzpatrick	Vagabond			
	Terence Reilly	Like			
	Tho. Fleming	Like)			
28 Aug 1742	Darby Foley	Like)			
	Charles Toole	Like)			
	Mary Byrne	Like)	72	0	0
26 Mar 1743					
8 Aug 1743	Edmond Cavanagh	Grand Larceny	20	0	0
			192	0	0

30

Assizes Dates	Persons ordered for transportation	Crimes	Money presented for that purpose
			L s d
7 Apr 1737			
28 Jul 1737			
27 Mar 1738	Darby Ryan	Vagabond	
	Walter Butler	Like	
	John Reddy	Like	
	James Doran	Like	
22 Jul 1738	Patrick Kelly	Like)	
	Andrew Dargan	Like)	
	Bryan McGuire	Like)	
	Dennis Ryan	Like)	
	John Delany	Like)	
	Michael Kelly	Like)	
	Patrick Walsh	Like)	42 0 0
22 Mar 1738	Pierce Purcell	Like)	
	James Butler	Like)	
	Patrick Corkran	Like)	
	Wm. Donohoe	Like)	6 0 0
11 Aug 1739	Dennis Madden	Grand Larceny	
	John Fitzpatrick	Like	
	Thomas Deerin	Like	
2 Apr 1740	Bryan Hurly	Vagabond	
	Joseph Moran	Grand Larceny	
24 Jul 1740	Patrick Magher	Vagabond)	
	Patrick Farrell	Like)	
	Joan Reynard	Like)	
	Pierce Butler	Like)	40 0 0
26 Mar 1741	Michael Roth	Grand Larceny	
	Thady Currin	Like	
	Hugh Bambrick	Vagabond	
29 Jul 1742	John Comerford	Like	
	James Comerford	Like	
	Andrew Doyle	Like	
	Michael Mars	Grand Larceny	
	John Broderick	Grand Larceny	
	Patrick Dwyer	Like	
	Robert Nugent	Like	
	Rowland Bourk	Vagabond	

Cont'd

Assizes Dates	Persons ordered for transportation	Crimes	Money presented for that purpose		
			L	s	d
14 Apr 1742	Margaret Cavanagh	Grand Larceny)			
	Wm. Conway	Vagabond)			
	Darby Kennedy	Grand Larceny)	66	0	0
22 Aug 1742	Hugh McDaniell	Petty Larceny			
	Thomas Magrath	Like			
	Henry Bowles	Vagabond			
	Richard Fyann	Like			
30 Mar 1743	Richard Carroll	Grand Larceny)			
	Patrick Grace	Like)			
	Edmond Bryan	Like)			
	Thomas Kerry	Vagabond)			
	Timothy Carthy	Like)			
	Patrick Broder	Grand Larceny)			
11 Aug 1743					
			————————		
			182	0	0

COUNTY OF THE CITY OF KILKENNY

Assizes Dates	Persons ordered for transportation	Crimes	Money presented for that purpose		
			L	s	d
7 Apr 1737					
28 Jul 1737	Mary Morissy	Vagabond	6	0	0
27 Mar 1738					
19 Jul 1737	Tho. Carthy	Grand Larceny)			
	Mary Carthy	Like)			
	Eliz. Lacy	Like)	15	0	0
22 Mar 1737	Tho. Martin	Vagabond	5	0	0
	Roger Hart	Like	5	0	0
11 Aug 1739					
2 Apr 1740	Patrick Hosey	Grand Larceny	12	0	0
24 Jul 1740	Bryan Hogan	Vagabond			
	Connors Scanlon	Grand Larceny			
	James Dowling	Like			

Cont'd

Assizes Dates	Persons ordered for transportation	Crimes	Money presented for that purpose		
			L	s	d
26 Mar 1741	Gordan Neal	Like)			
	Thady Hesseran	Vagabond)	24	0	0
29 Jul 1741	Patrick Read	Grand Larceny	6	0	0
14 Apr 1742	Patrick Phelan	Vagabond	6	0	0
12 Aug 1742	Edmond Hoban	Like	6	0	0
30 Mar 1743	William Cody	Convicted of felony)			
11 Aug 1743		of death pardoned)			
		for transportation)6		0	0
			96	0	0

COUNTY OF WEXFORD

Assizes Dates	Persons ordered for transportation	Crimes	Money presented for that purpose		
			L	s	d
14 Apr 1737					
22 Jul 1737	Cornelius Madden	Vagabond)			
	Timothy McDaniell	Like)			
	Patrick Kenny	Like)	18	0	0
4 Apr 1738	William Ingerdall	Petty Larceny	32	8	1
15 Jul 1738	Francis Fitzgerald	Grand Larceny			
	Miles Peake	Like			
16 Mar 1738	Miles Darcy	Vagabond			
	John Murray	Grand Larceny			
	Mary Gill	Like			
	Daniel Murphy	Like			
17 Aug 1739	David Redmond	Vagabond)			
	Darby Redmond	Like)			
	William McCull	Grand Larceny)			
	Hannah Murphy	Vagabond)			
	Patrick Barry	Like)			
	William Stewart	Like)	18	0	0

Cont'd

33

Assizes Dates	Persons ordered for transportation	Crimes	Money presented for that purpose		
			L	s	d
10 Apr 1740	Patrick Palliser	Grand Larceny	30	9	4
19 Jul 1740	Maurice Kelly	Vagabond)			
	Miles Darcy	Like)	24	0	0
	Edmond Prendergast	Grand Larceny			
2 Apr 1741	Thomas Devereux	Petty Larceny)			
	Peter Hanton	Grand Larceny)			
	James Dunphy	Like)	30	0	0
23 Jul 1741	Isaac Foster	Grand Larceny)			
	George Kelly	Like)			
	James Doyle	Like)			
	Peter Dunn	Like)	18	0	0
21 Apr 1742	Benjamin Shaw	Vagabond)			
	James Fever	Like)	12	0	0
			182	17	0

6 Aug 1742	Twenty persons presented this assizes and ordered for transportation, but all drowned in their passage from Wexford to Dublin, therefore no money presented.

7 Apr 1743	Andrew Fortune	Grand Larceny
	Murtagh Doyle	Vagabond
	Laurence Connick	Like
17 Aug 1737	Patrick McDaniell	Grand Larceny
	James McDaniell	Like

COUNTY OF WICKLOW

Assizes Dates	Persons ordered for transportation	Crimes	Money presented for that purpose		
			L	s	d
19 Apr 1737	Thomas Jackson	Vagabond			
	Terence Byrne	Like			
	William Kenny	Like			
18 Jul 1737			10	0	0
10 Apr 1738	Edmond Boyne	Grand Larceny			
10 Jul 1738	James Genarty	Vagabond			
12 Mar 1738	John Deoghoe	Grand Larceny			
	Charles Byrne	Like			
23 Aug 1739			12	0	0
14 Apr 1740	Richard Dunn	Grand Larceny	6	0	0
15 Jul 1740	Michael Fitzharris	Vagabond			
9 Apr 1741	Hugh Lacey	Like			
	Patrick McAtee	Like			
	Patrick Durass	Like			
	Edmund Nowlan	Like			
	Morgan Byrne	Grand Larceny			
	George Cullen	Like			
	Daniel Keoghoe	Like			
17 Jul 1741	Patrick McCann	Like			
	Charles Kealy	Like			
	Edmund Kennedy	Like			
	Patrick Bourke	Like			
	Owen McDaniell	Like)			
27 Apr 1742	John Doyle	Vagabond)			
	Terence Murphy	Grand Larceny)			
	Richard Kerwan	Vagabond)	60	0	0
2 Aug 1742	Sarah Donelly	Petty Larceny			
12 Apr 1743	Margaret Nowlan	Grand Larceny)			
	James Byrne	Vagabond)			
	Michael Doyl	Petty Larceny)			
	Elizabeth Dunn	Vagabond)	72	0	0
23 Aug 1743	John McNamara	Like	23	0	0
			191	0	0

I do hereby certify that in the foregoing sheets are contained a list of all convict felons and vagabonds who have been ordered for transportation for these seven years last past, as also the several sums of money presented for those purposes in the several Counties of Kildare, King's County, Queen's County, Carlow, Kilkenny, County of the City of Kilkenny, Wexford and Wicklow, in the Province of Leinster.

Dated this nineteenth day of November 1743.

Thomas Kanning deputy Clerk of the Crown

COUNTY OF WESTMEATH

A list of all convicted felons and vagabonds who have been ordered for transportation for seven years last past in the several Counties of Westmeath and Longford in the north-west circuit of Ulster and province of Leinster.

Dates of the Assizes	Persons ordered for transportation	Crime	Money presented		
			L	s	d
14 Mar 1736-7			18	0	0
26 Sep 1737	Patrick Prendergast	Vagabond			
	James Donoghoe	Like			
	Daniel Daly	Like			
	James Mulligan	Like			
	James Blunt	Like			
	John Ward	Like			
	Michael Gray	Like			
	William Mulligan	Like			
6 Mar 1737	James Wheelaghan	Like			
	Cormick Murray	Like			
1 Aug 1738	John Connor	Like			
	Peter Carton	Like			
12 Mar 1738	Thomas Slevan	Like			
	Connor McDermott	Like			
	Jane Mathews	Grand Larceny			
	Ellenor Nugent	Like			
	Patrick McDermott	Vagabond			
	Patrick Flanagan	Like			
	John McAvoy	Like			
	Daniel McCarren	Like			
13 Aug 1739	Baldwin Potter	Like			
Cont'd	Peter Kelly	Like			

Dates of the Assizes	Persons ordered for transportation	Crimes	Money presented		
			L	s	d
	John Harrick	Like			
	George Macken	Like			
	Henry Dalton	Like			
	Michael Keatings	Like			
	Honor Molloy	Like			
	Ellenor Naughton	Like			
	Margaret Naughton	Like			
11 Mar 1739	Alex McDonnell	Grand Larceny			
31 Jul 1740	James McDonnell	Like			
11 Mar 1740	Ann Kean	Like			
5 Aug 1741	Francis Cassedy	Vagabond			
	Henry Dalton	Like			
	Dennis Heyland	Like			
	Patrick Nary	Like			
	James Dungan	Like			
	James Kelly	Like			
5 Aug 1741	Dennis Kelly	Like			
	Bryan Kelly	Like			
	Peter Bowen	Like			
	James Cavanagh	Like			
	James Finlay	Like			
	Miles Kearnan	Like			
22 Apr 1742	William Gibbons	Like			
	Hugh Slevin	Grand Larceny			
	Thomas Reilly	Vagabond)			
	Christopher Manny	Like)			
	John Hall	Like)			
	David Golding	Like)			
	Henry Hyland	Like)			
	Thady McManus	Like)			
	Andrew Manny	Like)			
24 Aug 1742	Laurence Whyte	Like)	64	0	0
	Roger Farrell	Grand Larceny	104	0	0
	Matthew McDonnell	Vagabond			
	Patrick McDonnell	Like			
	Peter Griver	Like			
1 Apr 1742	James Gordon	Grand Larceny	24	0	0
10 Aug 1743	Patrick Kearnan	Like	----------		
			270	0	0

Assizes Dates	Persons ordered for transportation	Crimes	Money presented for that purpose		
			L	s	d
22 Sep 1737			18	0	0
10 Mar 1737	Ellinor Power	Grand Larceny	6	0	0
7 Aug 1738	Patrick Slevin	Vagabond			
	Owen McCabe	Like			
	James Quin	Like			
21 Mar 1738	James McNahoe	Grand Larceny	4	0	0
20 Aug 1739			8	0	0
17 Mar 1739	Laurence Angley	Like			
4 Aug 1740				4	10
0					
10 Mar 1740					
10 Aug 1741	Thomas Needham	Vagabond			
	Patrick Nonan	Like			
	Patrick Brogan	Like			
	Thady Hanly	Petty Larceny			
	Patrick Mulledy	Vagabond			
17 Apr 1742	Patrick Kenny	Like	18	0	0
30 Aug 1742			12	0	0
20 Mar 1743					
16 Aug 1743			70	10	0

I do hereby cerify that in the foregoing sheets there are contained a list of all convict felons and vagabonds who have been ordered for transportation for these seven years last past, as also the several sums of money presented for those purposes in the Counties of Westmeath and Longford in the north-west circuit of Ulster, and province of Leinster.

Dated this nineteenth day of November 1743.

Thomas Kanning, dputy Clerk of the Crown.

COUNTY OF CORK

A list of the several convict felons and vagabonds ordered for transportation, for whom money was raised on the said County, and the several sums raised for that purpose for these seven years last past.

The Respective Assizes	Names of convicts, felons and vagabonds	Sums raised and to whom ordered	L
Lent Assizes 24 Mar 1736	John Dawley Cornelius Coughlan Richard Hagarty John Street Honor Crotty John Shaggareen als. Berry James English John Sullivan	Seventy pounds to William Delahoide	70
	Daniel Crowley Timothy Duane Joanna Carthy Charles Crowley John Connor Dennis Sullivan als. Cullitagh	Seventy pounds to William Delahoide	70
Same Assizes	William Connor Patrick Roach	Eight pounds to William Street	8
Summer Assizes 1 Aug 1737		No money presented	
Lent Assizes 18 Mar 1737-8 Summer Assizes 25 Jul 1738	Timothy Carthy Owen Sheehy Bartholomew Garalaght John Bryan Patrick Gould Thomas Walsh Timothy Shea Samuel Prince Michael Nunane	Fifty-four pounds to William Sullivan	54

Cont'd

39

The Respective Assize	Names of convicts felons and vagabonds	Sums raised	
Same Assizes	John Bennet Mary Fitzgerald	Four pounds to Samuel Lowthen	4
Lent Assizes 10 Apr 1739 Lent Assizes	Timothy Connell John Murphy Mary Bryan John Murhahy Robert Morcarty James Kelly	Twenty-one pounds to Robert Williamson for these and the foregoing three	21
Same Assizes	Philip Hauraham James Pickett William Roach	Twelve pounds to John Baldwin	12
Summer Assizes 16 Aug 1739		No money presented	
Lent Assizes 22 Mar 1739-40		No money presented	
Summer Assizes 29 Jul 1740		No money presented	
Lent Assizes 17 Mar 1740		No money presented	
Summer Assizes 27 Jul 1741	James Kelly John Harrington Mary Fitzgerald Dennis Carty Catherine Hamilton Teigue Bryen John Ryan Pete Murphy Daniel Culane Timothy Connell John Murphy Margaret Crimmeen Matthew Bright John Merrihy	Fifty-four pounds to Robert Williamson	

Cont'd

The Respective Assizes	Names of convicts felons and vagabonds	Sums raised	L
	Mary Bryan		
	John Lemmee		
	Robert Moriarty		
	Darby Murphy		54
Same Assizes	Margaret Sullivan	Fifty pounds to	
	Thomas Adams	ditto	
	James Mahony		
	Darby Driscoll		
	John Carthy		
	Timothy Leary		
	John sullivan		
	Nathaniel Williams		
	Pierce Butler		
	Chatherine Barrett		
	Philip Murphy		
	John Smith		
	Cornelius Crimmeen		
	John Long		50
Lent Assizes	Timothy Murphy	One hundred and fifty-	
	David Dillane	five pounds to Robert	
	Richard Hennesy	Travers	
	Catherine Buchilly		
	Joan Nichane		
	Malachi Madden		
	Daniel Hagarty		
	James Connell		
	als. John Sheehan		
	Dennis Crowley		
	Edmund Mulcahy		
	Owen Hickey		
	Daniel Murphy		
	John Shealy		
	William Johnson		
	Timothy Dawly		
	Michael Forrest		
	Teigue Murphy		
	Charles Regan		
	Daniel Sullivan		

Cont'd

The Respective Assizes	Names of convicts felons and vagabonds	Sums raised	L
	Daniel Donovan		
	Michael Coskry		
	John Sheelan		
	Dennis Mullane		
	Michael Murphy		
	Dennis Commane		
	Dennis Bryen		
	John Roache		
	Thomas Sheehan		
	Maurice Spillane		
	Timothy Coskry		
	John Bourke		155
Summer Assizes 20 Aug 1742		No money presented	
Lent Assizes 18 Mar 1742-43	Darby Mahony	Sixty pounds to	
	Dennis Driscoll	Robert Williamson	
	Patrick Sheehan		
	Ellenor Sullivan		
	Cornelius Donahoe		
	Daniel Scannell		
	John Connor		
	Timothy Regan		
	Timothy Donohoe		
	David Condon		
	Timothy Carroll		
	John Ronan		
	Michael Holland		
	Thomas Fitzgerald		
	Patrick Rayne		60
Summer Assizes 9 Aug 1743	Patrick Lynchy	Eighty pounds to	
	Cornelius Grany	Robert Williamson	
	Maurice Killigott		
	John Connor		
	Patrick Lewis		
	Daniel Bryan		
	Darby Collins		
	John Barry		

Cont'd

The Respective Assizes	Names of convicts felons and vagabonds	Sums raised	L
	John Donoghoe		
	Nicholas Kearny		
	Julian Murphy		
	Ellenor Cahane		
	Ellenor Roache		
	Elizabeth Ivers		
	Catherine Sullivan		
	Margaret Linnahane		
	Ellenor Ginnanane		
	Margaret Jones		
	Catherine Harrington		
	Mary Shannahane		80
		Total	566

COUNTY OF CORKE. To wit.
I certify that this is a true list of all convict felons and vagabonds ordered for transportation for these seven years last past, and that the sums in said list were raised for those purposes.

Dated this thirteenth day of December 1743.
John Purdon, Clk, Cor.

CITY AND COUNTY OF THE CITY OF CORKE

A list of all convict felons and vagabonds who have been ordered for transportation in and for the City of Corke for these seen years last past, with an account of what money hath been raised for those purposes.

At a general assizes and general goal delivery held for the County of said City the twenty-fifth of August 1736.

Elizabeth Keefe als. Lynchy
Julian Croneen
James Barrett
Darby Lyne
Tim. Sullivan als. Randam   Convict Felons

Cont'd

43

John Collins
William Fitzgerald
Dan. Hennelly als. Duff   Presented by the grand jury as
Susanna Crowly   vagabonds

At the same assizes, the sum of thirty pounds was raised and ordered to
be paid for William Delahoide for transporting to America:

John Fitzgerald
James Murphy
Daniel Donovan
Margaret Donohoe
Joan Croneen als. Murphy   Six felons convicted at the
Thomas Dyer als. John Keef   former assizes

At a Session of Oyer and Terminer held for the County of said City the
eighteenth of November, 1736.

John Vaughan
Mary Bastard
Jane Carroll
Mary Minister
John Godfrey als. Magrath
Rickard Donovan
Ann Murphy als. Lombard
Julian Sullivan
Michael als. William Kent
John Murphy   Felons convict

Bryan Carrick
Darby Cleary   Presented as vagabonds

At an assizes held the twenty-fourth of March 1736.

Maurice Bryan als. Gillane
Philip Daunt the elder
Cont'd
Phil. Daunt the younger
Mary Daunt
Dennis Kelly   Felons convict

44

The same assizes the sum of seventy three pounds ten shillings was raised and ordered to be paid to William Delahoide for transporting to America: Mary Bastard, Mary Minister, John Godfrey als. Magrath, Rickard Donovan, Julian Croneen, James Barrot, Darby Lyne, Timothy Sullivan als. Randam, William Fitzgerald, John Crawly, Bridget Kennelly, Michael Eyers, Daniel Kennelly, John Collins, Susannah Crowley, William Lyne als. Lyons, Henry Jacques, John Sullivan, Ann Murphy als. Lombard, Julian Sullivan and Michael, otherwise William Kent, twenty-one felons and vagabonds.

At an assizes held the fifth of August 1737.

John Mortimore
James Twomey
George Stanley
Mary Guily   Presented as vagabonds

At the same assizes the sum of three pounds ten shillings was raised and ordered to be paid to John Baldwin for transporting to American Maurice Bryan als. Gillane, a felon convicted at the last assizes, and seventeen pounds ten shillings raised to be paid William Delahoide for transporting Bryan Carrick, Phil. Daunt the elder and younger, and Mary Daunt and Dennis Kelly.

At an assizes held the eighteenth of March 1737.

Catherine the wife of	Convicted of Perjury and ordered
James Murphy	to be transported
Barbara Bourke	
Joan Browne	Convict felons
Patrick Byrne	
Joan Wheeler	
James Barron	
Ellen Connor als. Reaper	
Joan Lynchy	Presented as vagabonds

At the same assizes the sum of fourteen pounds was raised and ordered to be paid to William Ricketts for transporting to America John Murphy, John

Vaughan, George Stanley and Mary Guily, four felons and vagabonds under rules of transportation.

At an assizes held the twenty-fifth of July 1738.

Den. Dahony als. Saxon
Winifred Kelly
Miles Sweeny   Convict felons

John Parker als. Flanagan   Presented as a vagabond

At the same assizes the sum of thirteen pounds fifteen shillings was raised and ordered to be paid to Horatio Townsend, Esq, for transporting to America, Barbara Bourke, Joan Browne, Catherine the wife of James Murphy, James Barron and Patrick Byrn, under rules of transportation the last assizes.

At an assizes held the tenth of April 1739.

Mary Harrington
Rose Nagle
Cornelius Donoghoe
Thomas Keareen
John Kelly
William Fitzgerald   Convict felons
William Knockins
Ann McDaniel   Presented as vagabonds

At the same assizes the sum of twelve pounds was raised and ordered to be paid to John Baldwin, Esq, for transporting to America Winnefred Kelly, Miles Sweeny and Dennis Mahony als. Saxon, felons convicted at the last assizes.

At an assizes held the sixteenth of August 1739.

Maurice Heas
Timothy Deashiah
Ellenor Mohony   Convict felons

Mary Ryan als. Sweeny
Margaret Fitzgerald als. Ryan
Patrick Ryan
William Ryan   Presented as vagabonds

At an assizes held the twenty-second of March 1739.

Margaret Hurly
George Armstrong
William Sexton
Florence Carthy
Elizabeth Carroll   Convict felons

John Boyle als. Bryan
John Finally   Presented as vagabonds

At the same assizes the sum of thirty-seven pounds was raised and
ordered to be paid to Robert Williamson for transporting to America
Timothy Denashiah, Mary Ryan, Margaret Ryan, William Ryan, Maurice Heas,
Ellenor Mahony, William Knockins, Mary Harrington, Rose Nagle, Cornelius
Donoghoe, Thomas Keareen, John Kelly and William Fitzgerald, felons and
vagabonds under rules of transportation.
At an assizes held the twenty-ninth of July 1740:

Owen Callaghan
Call. McCallaghan
Joan Lynch   Convict felons

Joan Coleman
Richard Seehane
Thomas Healy   Presented as vagabonds

47

At an assizes held the seventeenth of March 1740:

Catherine Sweeny, Ellenor Kealiner, Elizabeth Murphy, Honor Scannell, Ellenor Magher, Mary Hickey als. Meany, als. Jane Hicks, Julian Purcell.

All being in custody under sentence of death for divers felonies by them committed, and being reprieved for several years past, at this assizes, severally pleaded his Majesty's pardon conditionally to be transported, and they were ordered to be transported accordingly.

Michael Collins
Morgan Gallery
Lewis Leary   Convict felons

Garret Connor als. Bane
John Lee
Margaret Bush
Margaret Healy als. Bryan
Roger Connor   Presented as vagabonds

At the same assizes the sum of thirty-five pounds were raised and ordered to be paid to George Fuller the younger and William Clarke, Esqs, Sheriffs for transporting to America, Ellenor Kealiher, Elizabeth Murphy, Honor Cavenagh als. Welsh, Honor Scannell, Ellenor Magher, Mary Hickey als. Meany als. Jane Hicks and Julian Purcell, felons under rules of transportation.

At an assizes held the twenty-seventh of July 1741.

Maurice Fitzgerald
Ellenor Dawley   Convict felons

Owen Calloghty als. Kilty
John Scannel the elder
John Scannel the younger
George Austen
Patrick Raines   Presented as vagabonds

At the same assizes the sum of three pounds was raised and ordered to be paid George Fuller the younger, Esq, one of the Sheriffs, for transporting to American Catherine Sweeny who was under the rule of transportation, and also the sum of seventy-five pounds sterling, was presented and ordered to be paid Robert Williamson, for transporting to American Michael Collins, Lewis Leary, Garet Connor, John Lee, Roger Connor, Cornelius Sheehan, Margaret Bryan, Margaret Bourke, Morgan Gallery, Cornelius Donaghoe, Thomas Keareen, John Kelly, William Fizgerald, Owen Callaghan, Callaghan MacCallaghan, Joan Lynch, John Coleman, Richard Sheehane, William Sexton, Elizabeth Carroll, Joan Field, Margaret Hurly, John Bryan, George Armstrong and Florence Carthy, who were under rules of transportation.

At an assizes held the thirty-first of March 1742:

Jeremiah Mahony
Cat. Dogherty als. Prendergast
Bridget Clarke
James Sinnick John Shinnick
Dennis McCarthy
Charles Carthy   Convict felons

John Henessy
Barthol. Bourke
Edmond Keane
Darby Madden
Charles Sullivan
Richard Flemming
Mary Benson   Presented as vagabonds

At the same assizes the sum of twenty-eight pounds was raised and ordered to be paid to Robert Travers, Esq, for transporting to America, John Scannell the elder, John Scannell the younger, Owen Culloghty, George Austen, Pat. Raines, Maurice Fitzgerald and Ellenor Dawley, who were under rules of transportation.

At an assizes held the sixteenth of August 1742:

John Lynchy
James Bryan als. Sowny
John Dawly   Convict felons

John Mahony   Presented as a vagabond

At the same assizes the sum of fifty-six pounds was raised and ordered to be paid to Robert Travers, Esq, for transporting to America, Jeremiah Mahony, Catherine Doherty als. Prendergast, Bridget Clarke, James Shinnick, John Shinnick, Dennis McCarthy, Charles Carthy, John Hennessy, Barth. Bourke, Edmond Keane, Richard Flemming, Charles Sullivan, Darby Madden and Mary Benson, who were under rules of transportation.

At an assizes held the eighteenth of March 1742:

John Dwyer   Convict felon

Barthol. Kelly
Anstace Owens als. Gow
Margaret Middleton wife Barrett
John Crocen
John Ryan
John Darrag   Presented as vagabonds

At an assizes held the ninth of August 1743:

John Macknamara
Philip Corkeran
Joan Barrett
Catherine Lycett   Convict felons

At the same assizes the sum of twenty-four pounds was raised and ordered to be paid to Robert Williamson for transporting to America, John Mahony, John Dawly, John Dwyer, James Bryan, John Lynchy and John Murphy, who were ordered to be transported at a former assizes.

COUNTY OF THE CITY OF CORKE
Russell Wood, gentleman, deputy Clerk of the Crown of the City of Corke, this day made oath before me that he hath made diligent search amongst the records of the Crown office of the said City, and that the foregoing list is, to the best of his judgment and belief, a true and full list of all and every the convict felons and vagabonds who have been ordered for transportation within the said City for these seven years past, with a true and full account of what money hath been raised for those purposes. Sworn before me at the City of Corke the twenty-ninth day of November 1743.   Randall Wesstrop, May

CITY AND COUNTY OF THE CITY OF LIMERICK

A list of all convict felons and vagabonds who were ordered for transportation out of the County of the City of Limerick, with an account of the money raised for those purposes.

L

John Brenan	Felon	To sheriffs for transporting	
Bridget Shanahan	Felon	three persons	17
Edward Charlton	Vagabond	To them for transporting	
Edward Hammon	Vagabond	Edward Charleton	5
William Lynch	Vagabond	To them for transporting two	
Same, Edward Charleton		persons	12
on a return		To them for transporting David	
David Glassan	Felon	Glassen	6
John Kean	Felon	To them for transporting two	
John Hennessy	Vagabond	persons	12
Thomas Conners	Felon	To them for transporting three	
Patrick Higgins	Felon	persons	9
Honour Campbell	Felon		—
			16

Search being made amongst the pleas of the Crown in the Crown-office of the City and County of the City of Limerick, I find that the twelve persons in the foregoing schedule mentioned, have been, at the several assizes held for the said City and County of the said City within seven years before the tenth day of November instant, ordered to be transported into some of his Majesty's plantations in America, and that the several sums in the other schedule before mentioned, amounting to sixty-one pounds Sterling, were within the time aforesaid ordered to be raised on the said City and County of the said City for transporting the said felons and vagabonds, which I certify this sixth day of December, 1743.

George Peacock, deputy Clerk of the Crown.

COUNTY OF LIMERICK

A list of all convict felons and vagabonds transported from the County of Limerick for the seven years before the tenth day of November 1743 with an account of the several sums paid for their transportation.

Assizes eleventh of April 1737
Assizes twentieth of July 1737:

Honor Rierdan	Felon
Thomas Lynch	Felon
Catherine Brien	Felon

Assizes seventh of April 1738:

John Neal	Felon
Honor Haly	Felon
Thomas Orchard	Felon
Mary Neal	Felon
James Collopy	Vagabond
Patrick Conners	Vagabond

Assizes twelfth of July 1738:

James Fitzgerald	Felon
Gillen Shea	Vagabond
Catherine Carty	Vagabond
Catherine Dawley	Vagabond
Daniel Callaghan	Vagabond

Assizes twenty-eighth of March 1739:

Brian Carrol als. Oultagh	Felon
Joan Barry	Felon
Timothy Knavin	Vagabond
Catherine Knavin	Felon
James Courcey	Felon
Laurence English	Vagabond
Mary English	Vagabond
Owen Hogan	Vagabond
Edmond Wade	Vagabond
Terence Fogarty	Felon

Assizes fourth of September 1739:

John Russell	Vagabond
Joseph Kirk	Felon
Edmond Power	Vagabond
Sarah Ryan als. Dulagh	Vagabond

Assizes ninth of April 1740
Assizes sixteenth of July 1740:

Mary Sullivan	Felon

Assizes fourth of March 1740:

Owen Cleary	Vagabond

Summer Assizes 1741:

William Rourke	Vagabond
Cornelius Callaghan	Felon

Assizes twenty-second of April 1742

John Ready	
John Farrell	
John Dwyer	Felon
John Gaffney	Vagabond
James Helay	Vagabond
Darby Hannon	Vagabond
Connor O'Conner	Felon
Maurice Commane	Felon
Connor Caffoe	Felon
Maurice Gibbon	Vagabond
Thomas Fraly	Vagabond
Daniel Nealan	Vagabond
Thomas Nealan	Vagabond
Francis Tracy	Vagabond
Honora Connel	Felon
Daniel Hickie	Vagabond
James Hessernan	Vagabond
Joan Sheaghan	Felon
Cont'd	

Laurence Sheaghan	Vagabond
Michael Griffith	Vagabond
Ellenor Croneen	Vagabond
Maurice Stack	Vagabond

Summer Assizes 1742:

John Currane	Felon
John Cough als. Riery	Vagabond

Assizes seventeenth of April 1743:

Darby Daly	Vagabond
John Barragan	Felon
Edmond Doyle	Felon
Patrick Shea	Felon

	L	s	d
Assizes: 20 Jul 1737 To William Bourke Sub-sheriff, for repairing the goal, transporting two felons and erecting a gallows.	36	15	10
Assizes: 7 Apr 1738 To William Bourke Sub-sheriff, for gibetting Daniel Ready, transporting two persons and transmitting felons.	31	1	10
Assizes: 28 Mar 1739 To John Bourke late Sub-sheriff, for transporting several persons and transmitting several felons.	100	4	3
Assizes: 4 Sep 1739 To Hugh Massy Sub-sheriff, for transporting ten felons and vagabonds.	60	0	0
Assizes: 16 Jul 1740 To Peter Felan for transporting five felons and vagabonds, transmitting prisoners and erecting a new gallows.	50	0	0
Summer Assizes 1742 To William Bourke Sub-sheriff, for transporting twenty felons and vagabonds, transmitting prisoners and prosecuting constables.	60	0	0
	338	1	11

Search being made amongst the pleas of the Crown in the Crown-office of the County of Limerick, I find that at the several assizes held in and for the said County within seven years before the tenth day of November instant the sixty persons in the annexed schedule mentioned, were ordered to be transported into some of his Majesty's plantations in America as felons and vagabonds, and that the several sums in the above schedule mentioned, amounting to three hundred and thirty-eight pounds one shilling and eleven pence Sterling, were within the time aforesaid, ordered to be raised on the said County for transporting felons and vagabonds, and for the other services and uses to the said sums in the said schedule severally mentioned, which I certify this twenty-fourth day of November 1743.

George Peacocke, Dep. Cl. Cr.

COUNTY OF KERRY

A list of all convict felons and vagabonds who have been ordered for transportation in the County of Kerry for these seven years last past, with an account of what money hath been raised for those purposes, commencing April assizes 1736.

	L	s	d
Assizes 16 April 1736: Raised for transporting Maurice Savane and Thomas Savane felons convict, ordered for transportation.	9	18	7
Assizes 5 April 1737: For transporting, transmitting and guarding William Howran a felon convict, ordered for transportation.	6	10	0
For transporting James Stack, Charles Cowley, John Connor, Cornelius Shea and Joan Carthy, vagabonds, presented and ordered for transportation.	30	0	0
Assizes 26 Jul 1737: For transporting James Marshall and James Agherine, felons convict, presented for mercy and ordered for transportation.	10	0	0
Presented then for the charges for transmitting them	2	0	1
Assizes 18 Jul 1738: For transporting Owen Sweeny, John McLoughlin als. Oltagh and Darby Downey, felons convict, presented for mercy and ordered for transportation, and for charges of transmitting them.	18	18	8

55

Assizes 4 April 1739:
For transporting John McJeffry Connell and Daniel
Killeghane convicts, under the like order, and charges of
transmitting them.   14 10 10

Assizes 19 August 1739:
For transporting and charges of transmitting Daniel
Callaghan, Dennis Downey, John Bromebane and Ally
Noonane convicts under like order.   26   2   6

Assizes 22 Jul 1740:
For transporting Dennis Connor als. Gunskagh, Daniel
Frenighty, Thomas Doolin, Maurice Doolin, Darby Sullivan,
Charles Rahelly, Dennis Sweeny and Mary Griffin convicts
under like order.   40   0   0
For charges of transmitting them to Corke.   7 17   3

Assizes 11 Mar 1741:
For transporting Matthias Gallavan, Thomas Paradine,
Owen Ferris, Dermot Collity, Michael Collity, James
Bourke, Cornelius Donoghoe, Teigue Dinaghy and Daniel
Dinaghy convicts and vagabonds under like order.   45   0   0
Expenses of transmitting them.   8 19   6

Assizes 12 Aug 1741:
For transporting and charges of transmitting Patrick
Connor, Darby Connor, Timothy Connor, John Sullivan,
Dennis Sullivan, Dennis Spillane, James Mulcane and
John Stack als. Crosbie vagabonds presented and ordered
for transportation.   49 12   0

Assizes 5 Apr 1742:
For transporting Garret Joy, John Denneen, Hugh
Brosnehane, Thomas Bryan, John Hease, John Dillane,
Maurice Cullane, Florence Scannell and David Sheghane
vagabonds under like order.   55   0   0

Assizes 10 Aug 1742:
For transporting Daniel Buohilly, Daniel Breene, Thomas
Millone, John Bryan, Dennis Shea, Murtogh Shea, Timothy
Managheene, Daniel Quirk, Ellenor Mohill als. Quirk,
Cornelius Lyne and Cornelius Launy convicts and
vagabonds ordered for transportation.   55   0   (
Raised for expenses and charges of transmitting them. 11   1   (

Cont'd

56

Assizes 1 Apr 1743:
For transporting Morgan Sweeny , Ellenor Connor, Mary
Mansfield and Catherine Fitzgerald vagabonds ordered
for transportation.   20   0   0
Raised for charges and expenses of transmitting them.   <u>3   0   0</u>

Total money raised   <u>413   10   4</u>

Total persons transported   68

No money was presented for those purposes at the last assizes.
Dated the seventeenth of November 1743.
Francis Cashell, deputy Clerk of the Crown for the County of Kerry.

COUNTY OF TIPPERARY

A list of all convict felons and vagabonds who have been ordered for
transportation for these seven years last past, with an account of what
money hath been raised for these purposes on said County, to commence
the twenty-seventh of March 1736, to the thirtieth of July 1743,
inclusive.

John Fitzgerald
William Hamerton
John Herns
Teigue Bryan als. McJohn
Edmond Power
Catherine Leary als. Glisan
Roger Sheehy
John Proctor
Darby Spillane
John Flinn
Morgan Dogherty
John Reily
James Glissan
Edmond Flynn
Thomas Green
William Dwyer
James Blake
Michael Broder als. Broderick
Thomas Dehony
James Carrigan
Daniel Collins
Cont'd

Edmond Kinnesean
Edmond Bourke
Richard Powell
Anthony Dwyer
Morres Hylahan
Patrick Grady
Edmond Cummin
John Geagin
Michael Hackett
Connor Quin
John Fowley
William Armstrong
Margaret Bryan
Daniel Crawley
Catherine Nugent
Nicholas Blake
Michael Diwane
Darby Hylan
John Ryan
Daniel Lawler
Margaret Brien

Mary Davis
Edmund Kennedy
Maurice Bolan
James Prendergast
David Haly
James Flannigan
John English
Daniel Mooney
Patrick Byrn
Thomas Carew
James Slattery
John Heas
William Bolan
John Looby
John Marry
William Dunn
Philip Trassy
William Ryan als. Stuokagh
William Kennedy
Martin Cleary
Stephen Brien
William Meagher
Robert Shorthell
Edmund Bourke

Daniel Carthy
Dennis Brien
John Ryan
John Hackett
Thomas Hogan
Pierce Flannigan
Edward Hanlan
Teigue Hough
John Brown
Martin Carew
Darby Heas
Patrick Ryan
John Bolan
Patrick Dalton
Darby Slattery
John Ryan
Teigue Higgins
Thomas Nowlan
Edmund Meagher
Thomas Cleary
Daniel Mahony
Michael Hogan
Philip Hollaghan
William Haraghton

Search being made amongst the pleas of the Crown for the County of Tipperary, I find and certify that the several respective persons in the annexed schedule have been ordered for transportation as above set forth, and that the sum of three hundred and one pounds four shillings and six pence Sterling had been presented and raised on said County for that purpose.   Dated this ninth day of December 1743.

Samuel Waller, Clerk of the Crown for the County of Tipperary.

COUNTY OF WATERFORD

A list of the several convict felons and vagabonds ordered for transportation, for whom money was raised on the said County, and the several sums raised for that purpose for those seven years last past.

Respective Assizes	Names of convict felons and vagabonds ordered for transportation		
Lent assizes 14 Mar 1736-7	John Connor Thomas Corban Honor Cahane John Greene	Eighteen pounds to Beverly Usher and Henry Mason Esqs	18
Summer assizes 12 Aug 1737	Philip Cassoe	Five pounds to ditto	5
Lent assizes 6 Mar 1737-8	David Kelly Lewis Welsh Patrick Supple Daniel Bane als. Kennedy	Twenty pounds to ditto	20
Summer assizes 8 Aug 1738	No person presented for transportation		
Lent assizes 17 Mar 1738-9	John Condon Daniel Murphy Edmund Connor	Fifteen pounds to ditto	15
Summer assizes 6 Aug 1739	No persons presented for transportation		
Lent assizes 12 Mar 1739-40	Patrick Galavan Darby Dunn	No sum	
Summer assizes 11 Aug 1740	John Mulcahy Daniel Kearin Darby Mulcahy	Fifteen pounds to ditto	15
Lent assizes 6 Apr 1741	Hugh Tallon Michael Mulcahy Richard Power	Fifteen pounds to ditto	15

Cont'd

Respective Assizes	Names of convicts, felons and vagabonds ordered for transportation		
Summer assizes 15 Jul 1741	Maurice Norris James Tobin Michael Hallinan Darby Quinlan Edmund Costello John Bourke David Norris Darby Dooling John Egan Martin Fogarty	Fifty pounds to ditto	50
Lent assizes 17 Mar 1741-2	David Power Edmond Lynch John Scannell John Connell Patrick Cullue John Beacon Mary Crotty	Thirty-five pounds to ditto	35
Summer assizes 6 Sep 1742	Ellen Quirk Michael Whelan John Reilly	Fifteen pounds to ditto	15
Lent assizes 5 Mar 1742-3	John Fahy	Five pounds to	5
Summer assizes 27 Jul 1743	None presented for transportation nor no sums raised.		

Total   £183

COUNTY OF WEXFORD
I certifie that the above is a true list of all convict felons and vagabonds who have been ordered for tansportation for these seven years last past, and that the above sums were raised for those purposes.
Dated the 13th day of December, 1743.

John Purdon, Clk. Cor.

COUNTY OF THE CITY OF WATERFORD

A list of all convict felons and vagabonds ordered for transporation for these seven years last past, with an account of what money hath been raised for those purposes for those seven years last past.

Respective Assizes	Names of the convict felons and vagabonds ordered for transportation	Sums raised and to whom ordered	L
Lent assizes Respective Assizes	Edmund Roache Names of convict felons and vagabonds ordered for transportation		
14 Mar 1736-7	Patrick Grady	No money raised	
Summer assizes 12 Aug 1737	No person presented for transportation No money raised		
Lent assizes 6 Mar 1737-8	No person presented for transportation No money raised		
Summer assizes 8 Aug 1738	No person presented for transportation No money raised		
Lent assizes 17 Mar 1738-9	No person presented for transportation No money raised		
Summer assizes 6 Aug 1739	No person presented for transportation No money raised		
Lent assizes 12 Mar 1739-40	Darby Sullivan	Five pounds to Francis Barker and Wm. Price	5
Summer assizes 11 Aug 1740	No person ordered for transportation No money raised		
Lent assizes 6 Apr 1741	John Walsh Charles Banfield Daniel Noonan	Thirteen pounds to the Treasurer	13
	Thomas Hallinan Oth. Allinan Michael Keenan John Whelan	Five pounds to Francis Barker and William Price	5

61

Respective Assizes	Names of convicts, felons and vagabonds ordered for transportation	Sums raised and to whom ordered	L
Summer assizes 15 Jul 1741	Alice Payne Owen Cleary	Ten pounds to ditto	10
Lent assizes	No persons presented for transportation		
Respective Assizes	Names of convict felons and vagabonds ordered for transportation		
27 Mar 1741-2	No money presented		
Summer assizes 6 Sep 1742	No person presented for transportation No money presented		
Lent assizes 5 Mar 1742-3	Timothy Ryan Peter Moore	Ten pounds to Phineas Barret and Jeffrey Paul, Sheriffs	10
Summer assizes 27 Jul 1743	No person presented for transportation		
		Total	£53

CITY OF WATERFORD
I certifie that the above is a true list of all convict felons and vagabonds who have been ordered for transportation for these seven years last past, and that the above sums contained in said list were raised for those purposes.
Dated this 13th day of December 1743.

John Purdon, Clerk Crown.

COUNTY MONAGHAN

A list of all convict felons and vagabonds who have been ordered for transportation for these seven years last past in the several Counties of Monaghan, Armagh, Antrim, Downe, and the county of the town of Carrickfergus, with an account of what money hath been raised for those purposes.

Transportation order date	Name of convict	Crime	Money paid and to whom
Lent assize 1737	No transportations ordered		
Summer assize 1737	No transportations ordered		
Lent assize 1737	John Armstrong	Vagabond	£42
	Pat. McDonnell	Con. Felon	Richard Johnston
	Knogh. McCaffry	Vagabond	Esq
	John McEntee	Con. Felon	
	John Dogherty	Like	
	Con. McMahon	Like	
	Edward Harvey	Vagabond	
Summer assize 1738	Flan. Clerkin	Con. Felon	£48
	Phil. McNeny	Like	Nicholas Foster Esq
Lent assize 1739	Fennal Cullen	Felon	
	John Dollan	Like	
	Andrew Erwine	Vagabond	
Summer assize 1739	Anthony Murphy	Felon	
	Bryan Callan	Like	
	Dennis Sherry	Like	
Lent assize 1740	Henry Croan	Like	£18
	John McCroddan	Vagabond	Humphry Evat
	James Kelly	Felon	Esq
Summer assize 1740	Pat. O'Mullan	Like)	£48
	Bryan McQuade	Vagabond)	Francis
			) Richardson Esq
Lent assize 1741	John McDonnell	Felon)	
	Mary McMahon	Vagabond)	
	James Reilly	Like)	
		)	
Summer assize 1741	John Clark	Like)	
	Pat. McAtee	Like)	
	Mary Brattan	Like	£6 John
	Pat. Hughs	Vagabond	Standford Esq
	Joan Dennis	Felon	)£6 each
Lent assize 1742	Corm. Callaghan	Like	)Francis
	James Reilly	Like	)Richardson
Cont'd	Thomas Jones	Like	)

Transportation order date	Name of Convict	Crime	Money paid and and to whom
	Francis Byrn	Vagabond	£18
	Charles Linchy	Like	John Standford
	Ann Newton	Like	Esq
Summer assize 1742	No transportations ordered		
Lent assize 1743	James Steel	Felon	No money yet raised for
Summer assize 1743	James Dennis	Like	transportation
	John Nesbit	Vagabond	
		Total	£204

Examined by Edmund Fleming, deputy Clk. Cor.

COUNTY OF ARMAGH

Transportation order date	Name of convict	Crime	Money paid and to whom
Lent assize 1737	David Brown	Felon	No money raised
Summer assize 1737	No transportations ordered		
Lent assize 1737	Peter Staunton	Felon	£5 John McGeogh
Summer assize 1738	No transportations ordered		
Lent assize 1739	James McKenna	Felon	£5 Geo. Walker
	Pat. Hughs als. Parokagh Hughs	Vagabond	
Lent assize 1740	William Wilson	Like	£20 John
	William Fitzpatrick	Felon	Gilispie
	Sheela Day als. Robishaw	Like	
Summer assize	Cornelius Quinn	Like	£15 Edward Ohre
	Michael Murphy	Like	
	James Young	Like	
Cont'd	Neall Quinn	Vagabond	£5 Adam Noble

Transportation order date	Name of Convict	Crime	Money paid and to whom
Lent assize 1741	Hugh O'Neill	Felon	£15 Edward Ohre
	Ann Totall	Like	
	Henry Murray	Like	
Summer assize 1741	Joseph Wright	Like	£44 Adam Noble
	Manus Fegan	Vagabond	
	Terence Fegan	Felon	
Lent assize 1742	Pat. Campbell als. McCavill	Vagabond	
	Elizabeth Mercer	Felon	
	Arthur O'Fegan	Like	
Summer assize 1742	William Hunter	Like	
	John Keenan	Convicted of treason. Pardoned on condition of transportation.	
Lent assize 1743	Aeneas Collins	Forgery	£20 William Graham
	Ann Terrill	Felon	
	Pat. McAnalty	Like	
	Margaret Hagan	Like	
Summer assize 1743	Michael Sandell	Perjury	No money yet raised
	Mary Burns als. Kelly	Felon	
		Total	£129

Examined by Edward Fleming, deputy Clk. Cor.

COUNTY OF ANTRIM

Transportation order date	Name of convict	Crime	Money paid and to whom
Lent assize 1737	John Murray	Felon	£20 Hill Wilson
	Hugh Gibson	Like	
	William Williams	Like	
	John McBride	Like	
	Charles Price	Like	£5 Hill Wilson
Summer assize 1737	Henry McCashland	Vagabond	
	Robert McNeight	Like	
Lent assize 1738	John Shaw	Felon	£70
	James McIlvenan	Like	Edward Smith
	Richard O'Cahane	Vagabond	
	Derby O'Cahane	Like	
	Hugh Keery	Like	
	Robert Elliot	Like	
	Robert Allin	Like	
	William Waugh	Like	
	William Dixon	Like	
	William Forrest	Like	
	Samuel Kimmin	Felon	
	Neall McFarland	Like	
Summer assize 1738	John Poague	Like	£5 Edw. Smith
Lent assize 1739	William Bruce	Vagabond	£15
	James Longmore	Like	Davys Wilson
Summer assize 1739	Patrick Kerr	Felon	
	William Kelly	Felon	£30 Will. Boyd
	John Boyle	Vagabond	
Lent assize 1740	Ed. Morgan als. Giles	Felon	
	Matthew Farrel	Like	
	Alexander Steel	Like	
	Ann O'Neil	Like	
	Will. Patterson	Vagabond	£45 Will. Boyd
	James Patterson	Like	
	John Patterson	Like	

Cont'd

Transportation order date	Name of convict	Crime	Money paid and to whom
	Edward Leaths	Like	
	Charles McAuly	Like	
	Doug. McDonnell	Like	
	Oli. O'Houghian	Like	
	John O'Houghian	Felon	
	John Seely	Like	
Summer assize 1740	Neall McAuly	Like	£10 Will. Boyd
	Roger McBride	Vagabond	
Lent assize 1741	Andrew Beard	Like	£5 Conway Spencer
Summer assize 1741	Edward Ellis	Like	£30
	Adam Dean	Felon	Conway Spencer
	Arch. Lemond	Like	
	Robert Lemond	Like	
	Bryan-buy McAuly	Like	
	Joseph Neill	Like	
Lent assize 1742	Mary McElery	Like	£10
Summer assize 1742	Mary McElroy	Like	Felin O'Neill
	Ann Campbell	Like	£5 James Smart
Lent assize 1743	No transportations ordered		
Summer assize 1743	No transportations ordered		

Total   250

Examined by Edward Fleming, deputy Clk. Cor.

COUNTY DOWNE

Transportation order date	Name of convict	Crime	Money paid and to whom
Lent assize 1737	William Peden	Felon	£25
	William Erwine	Like	The Hon
	John Towel	Like	Arthur Hill
	Lawrence Wilson	Like	
	Mic. McMahon als.		
	Mathews	Like	
Summer assize 1737	Robert McCalls	Like	£45
	David McCalls	Felon	John Dunkin
Lent assize 1738	James Harper	Like	
	Michael Burns	Vagabond	
	Absalom Kettles	Like	
	Margaret Moreton	Felon	
	John Cassedy als.		
	John the rover als.		
	John Moor	Vagabond	
	Stumphy Bryan	Felon	
	Elizabeth Shaw	Perjury	£35
Summer assize 1738	John Kelly	Vagabond	Adam Browne
Lent assize 1739	William Laverto als.		
	Sacheveral	Like	
	Edward Murray	Felon	
	John Martin	Like	
	Thomas Kerr als.		
	Carran	Vagabond	
	Jane Shaw, elder	Like	
	Jane Shaw, younger	Like	) £25
			) George Walker
Summer assize 1739	Dennis Kearns als.		)
	McKearnan	Felon	)
	Mary McComb als.		)
	McCalls	Like	)
			)

Cont'd

Transportation order date	Name of convict	Crime	Money paid and to whom
Lent assize 1740	Hugh McClement	Felon)	
	Ellinor Quinlan	Vagabond)	
	Mary Butler	Felon)£25	
		)James Smart	
Summer assize 1740	Thomas Shepherd	Vagabond)	
	Patrick Doran	Felon)	
		)	
Lent assize 1741	John Bennet	Like)	
	James McKewin	Like)	
	Matthew Kane	Like	£5 James Smart
Summer assize 1741	John Cooper	Vagabond)£25	
		)James Echlin	
Lent assize 1742	William Bingham	Felon)	
	Patrick Hanvy	Like)	
	Phelemy Doran	Like)	
	Francis Fegan	Like)	
	James Orr	Like	
Summer assize 1742	No transportations ordered		
Lent assize 1743	John Watterson	Felon	£15
	John Young	Vagabond	Adam Browne
	Thomas Taylor	Felon	
Summer assize 1743	John Boyd	Vagabond	No money yet
	John Bartley	Like	raised
		Total	£200

COUNTY OF THE TOWN OF CARRICKFERGUS

No convict felons or vagabonds ordered for transportation for these seven years last past.

County of Monaghan	£	204	
County of Armagh		129	
County of Antrim		250	
County of Downe		200	
Total	£	783	

Examined by Edward Fleming, deputy Clk. Cor.

A list of all convicted felons and vagabonds who have been ordered for transporation for seven years last past in the several Counties of Cavan, Fermanagh, Tyrone, Donegall, and City and County of Londonderry.

COUNTY OF CAVAN

Date of assizes	Persons ordered for transportation	Crime	Money presented
19 Aug 1743 25 Mar 1743	Miles Reilly	Vagabond	£ 12
2 Sep 1742	Isaac Byrne	Vagabond	£ 30
14 Apr 1742	Timothy Smith John Lynchy Bryan Daly Edmond Donnelly Owen Smith	Vagabond Like Like Grand Larceny Like	£10
13 Aug 1741	John Sheridan Edmond Hanlon Daniel McGuire	Like Petty Larceny Grand Larceny	£ 41
19 Mar 1740	John Duffy John Johnston John Dawson Phelim Reilly John Mulligan	Vagabond Like Petty Larceny Vagabond Grand Lrceny	
7 Aug 1740	Patrick Cummin	Like	£ 24

Cont'd

70

Date of assizes	Persons ordered for transportation	Crime	Money presented
20 Mar 1739	Daniel Carmety	Like	
23 Aug 1739	Mary Clancey	Like	
24 Mar 1738	Patrick Jones	Vagabond	
10 Aug 1738	Owen Loughran	Like	£ 36
14 Mar 1737	John Fitzpatrick	Like	
	Margaret Brady	Like	
24 Mar 1737	Isabella McDermot	Like	
	Terence Fitzpatrick	Like	
	Philip Barry	Like	
	William Watson	Grand Larceny	
19 Sep 1737	Bryan Gargan	Vagabond	
	Bartholomew Byrne	Like	
22 Mar 1736	Rose Johnston	Grand Larceny	
	James Hussey	Vagabond	
		Total	£153

COUNTY OF FERMANAGH

Date of Assizes	Persons ordered for transportation	Crime	Money presented
22 Aug 1742			
23 Mar 1743			
7 Sep 1742			
10 Apr 1742	Simon Cassedy	Vagabond	£30
	Edmond McLoughlin	Like	
	Robert Graham	Like	
	Turlagh Mulvurnagh	Like	
	Christopher Barry	Like	

Cont'd

Date of assizes	Persons ordered for transportation	Crime	Money presented
17 Aug 1741	John McDade	Grand Larceny	
	Francis McMelty	Vagabond	
23 Mar 1740	Peter Lamin	Like	£18
11 Aug 1740	Owen McCaffry	Like	
	Charles McManus	Grand Larceny	
25 Mar 1740			
27 Aug 1739			
29 Mar 1739			£30
15 Aug 1738	William Henderson	Vagabond	
	Bryan McGuire	Like	
	John Armstrong	Like	
	Thomas Armstrong	Like	
	Maurice Cassidy	Like	
18 Mar 1737			£18
24 Sep 1737	John Oneil	Grand Larceny	
	James Magolrick	Like	£14
26 Mar 1737	Francis McNeill	Like	
	Owen Bannon	Vagabond	
	Thomas Bannon	Like	
	Terence o'Caddin	Like	
		Total	£110

COUNTY OF TYRONE

Date of Assizes	Persons ordered for transportation	Crime	Money presented
26 Aug 1743	Robert Mullan	Vagabond	
17 Mar 1742			
10 Sep 1742	Margaret Sally	Like	£45
6 Apr 1742	Paul o'Brillaghan	Like	
	Arthur McCourt	Like	

Cont'd

Date of Assizes	Persons ordered for transportation	Crime	Money presented
	Patrick Sharky	Like	
	Hugh o'Brien	Like	
	Charles McCowell	Sheep stealing	
	Edmund McCowell	Sheep stealing	
20 Aug 1741	Roger o'Neil	Vagabond	£72
	James McCullagh	Like	
26 Mar 1741	Henry Keenan	Like	
	Henry McQuade	Like	
	Bryan McQuade	Like	
	Roger McQuade	Like	
	Michael McCowell	Like	
	Patrick McQuade	Like	
14 Aug 1740	Henry Allen	Like	
	Catherine Burns	Like	
	Patrick o'Kain	Vagabond	
	Philip o'Haghy	Cow stealing - presented for mercy	
27 Mar 1740	James Darcy	Vagabond	
	Dunkan Keenan	Like	
	John Lawson	Like	
	Andrew Mills	Like	
	Robert Mills	Like	
	Cornelius Gormly	Grand Larceny	
31 Aug 1739	Hugh Meane	Like	£15
2 Apr 1739			
18 Aug 1738	Shane o'Quin	Vagabond	
	Francis McGourk	Like	
	Hugh McGourk	Like	
	James McGourk	Like	
22 Mar 1737	Neil McGittigan	Like	
	Knogher o'Quin	Like	
	Charles Donelly	Like	

Cont'd

Date of Assizes	Persons ordered for transportation	Crime	Money presented
9 Sep 1737	John Gallagher	Like	£15
	Bryan o'Divin	Like	
13 Mar 1737	Neely McGirr	Like	
	James McCabe	Like	
	Edmond mcRoddin	Like	
	James McCullagh	Like	
	Mary Mitchell	Grand Larceny	
		Total	£156

COUNTY OF DONEGAL

Date of Assizes	Persons ordered for transportatiton	Crime	Money presented
31 Aug 1743	Daniel McMahon	Vagabond	
	James Flanagan	Like	£25
	Bridget Flanagan	Like	
14 Mar 1742			
15 Sep 1742			£20
2 Apr 1742	Michael Conolly	Vagabond)	£100
	William Caldwell	Like)	
	Adal Steel	Grand Larceny)	
	John Gallagher	Like)	
5 Aug 1741	Charles o'Donnell	Like	
	Toal o'Boy	Like	
	Michael o'Quin	Grand Larceny	
	James McLoughlin	Like	
	Phelemy Cairney	Like	
	Dennis Murry	Like	
	Teigue o'Kelly	Like	
	Hugh McNamee	Like	
	James Scanlon	Like	
	Mary Gillispie	Like	
	Edmond o'Dogherty	Vagabond	

Cont'd

74

Date of Assizes	Persons ordered for transportation	Crime	Money presented
31 Mar 1737	Patrick o'Conolly	Like	
	Patrick o'Donnel	Like	
	James Dunbarr	Like	
	Patrick Mooney	Grand Larceny	
	Hugh-buy oGallagher	Like	
19 Aug 1740	Fergal McCoart	Vagabond	£20
	Fergal Cullin	Grand Larceny	
	Michael McCoart	Vagabond	
	Owen Galdanagh	Like	
	Constantine o'Donnell	Like	
2 Apr 1740	Rose McGuire als. Smith	Grand Larceny	
	Mary Gallagher	Like	
	Charles o'Dogherty	Vagabond	
	Charles o'Boyle	Like	
5 Sep 1739	Neal Mergagh McSwine	Like	
6 Apr 1739	Joseph McFarland	Grand Larceny	
	Thomas Johnston	Like	
	Dudley Gallagher	Vagabond	
23 Aug 1738			£15
27 Mar 1738	Charles o'Gallagher	Like	
	Robert Irwin	Like	
	James Lorcan	Like	
	Hugh Gallagher	Like	
6 Sep 1737			£45
4 Apr 1737	William Carey	Like	
	George Stinson	Like	
			————
		Total	£240

CITY AND COUNTY OF LONDONDERRY

Date of Assizes	Persons ordered for transportation	Crime	Money presented
3 Sep 1743			£30
10 Mar 1742	Arthur o'Mullan	Vagabond	
	Randal McDonnell	Like	
	Charles Shannon	Like	
	John McGeogh	Like	
18 Sept 1742			
30 Mar 1742	John McGlosky	Grand Larceny	£12
	James McGinnis	Vagabond	
28 Aug 1741	James McEnorland	Grand Larceny	£30
	Owen o'Madigan	Like	
3 Apr 1741	Shane Braddagh o'Cahen	Vagabond	
	Henry Murray	Like	
	William Harrower	Like	
	John Armstrong	Like	
	Dennis Quigley	Like	
	Patrick McRory	Like	
	Henry o'Hagan	Like	
	Bryan Conolly	Like	
	Art o'Larkin	Like	
	John Dogherty	Like	
	John Hasson	Like	
	Edmond Gallagher	Grand Larceny	
	Fergal Gallagher	Petty Larceny	
	Henry o'Donaghy	Like	
	John Hamilton	Like	
22 Aug 1740			
5 Apr 1740	Patrick Cherry	Vagabond	
	Patrick o'Cahan	Like	
8 Sep 1739			£24
10 Apr 1739			
26 Aug 1738	Samuel Carr	Vagabond	£15
	Dunkan o'Higgin	Like	
	Charles o'Harny	Grand Larceny	

Cont'd

76

Date of Assizes	Persons presented for transportation	Crime	Money presented
30 Mar 1738	John Halfpin	Vagabond	
	John McLoughlin	Like	
	John McDonnell	Grand Larceny	
	Daniel Lunchanan	Like	
	Mary o'Neil	Petty Larceny	
1 Sep 1737	Bryan McGlinn	Vagabond	
7 Apr 1737	John Ross	Like	
	James McDead	Like	
	Phelemy o'Mullan	Vagabond	
	Patrick Mulhollan	Like	
	George Stewart	Like	
	Peter McAnurlan	Like	
	John McGonigal	Grand Larceny	
26 Apr 1736	John Boy	Like	
	Margaret Wrot	Vagabond	____
		Total	£161

The foregoing papers are a fair abstract of the prisoners transported, and sums presented in the foregoing Counties for seven years, which I humbly certify, this fourteenth of November 1743.

George Taasse.

A list of the several convict felons and vagabonds who have been ordered for transportation in the several Counties of the province of Connaught from Summer assizes 1735, to Summer assizes 1743, inclusive, together with an account of what money hath been raised in that time for transporting such felons and vagabonds.

COUNTY OF GALWAY

Edmond Cranally
Catherine McDonnell als. O'Brien
Thady Hoghegan
Humphry Nelan
William Bourke
Michael Fahy
David Fitz Gibbon
William Shunaghane
Owen Ridican
Patrick Bourke
Hugh Dunn
James Dalton
John Cahan
John Lynch
Laughlin o'Loughlin
Richard Welsh
Patrick Kennedy
Thady Martin
Dennis Daly
John Daly
Michael Carr
Darby Farrell

John Ryan
Thomas Flaherty
John Kelly
Thomas Donaghoe
Thady Mullally als. Lally
Honora Coan
Mary Lavendar
Mortagh Mooney
Catherine Casey
Patrick Shaghnassy
Anthony St Leger
Thomas Linaghane
Francis Spencer
Richard Lawless
Catherine Hinagan
Michael Keighry
Murtogh Dermody
Augustine McCarra
John Shaghnassy
John Farrell
John Moran

COUNTY OF THE TOWN OF GALWAY

Thomas White

William Burne

COUNTY OF LEITRIM

Edmond Durk als. Lahy
Gregory McIles
Shane o'Bourke
Mable McCarty
Bryan McWeeny
Martin Molloy
James McKeon
Bryan McSharry
Michael Kenny
Bryan Reilly

Charles Costelloe
Thady Logan
Patrick McGlinn
Luke Neilan
Bryan Kelly
William Wilson
Thomas McSharry
Thomas Sumaghan
  als. Cullnagh
Dennis Kelly

78

COUNTY OF MAYO

Edmond Monnelly
David Roach
William McDonnough
Daniel Daver
Peter Greeve

James Farrell
William McConnogh
Hugh Magratli
Morgan Brislane

COUNTY OF ROSCOMMON

Bryan Monaghan
James Heany
Thomas McDonnell
Teigue McGreevy
Thady Flynn
Matthew McDonnell
Edward Phipps
Patrick Flanegan
Patrick McPadden
Bryan Miraghan
Bryan Kenny
Thady Lyons
Michael Denicon

George Coghran
Patrick Neiraghane
Thady Kelly
Alexander McDonnell
William Garvey
Bryan Coyne
John Naughton
Michael Bourke
Owen Rourke
William Griffin
Andrew McHugh
Garret Caghy

COUNTY OF SLIGOE

Henry Bruen
Rosanne Harcan
John Farrell als. Fanly als. Fitzgerald
Bridget Harcan
John Mullican
James Conolly
John Gallway als. Gallagher
John Gawny
John Reilly

John Mackey als. Johnins
Michael Connelly
William Bourke
Dennis Higgins
Daniel Coser als. Cogher
Dennis Gilmartin
Patrick Jordan
Loughlin Cugly
Patrick Cosly

COUNTY OF GALWAY

Summer assizes 1736, six pounds presented and paid to William Turvin, Esq, late High-sheriff, for transporting Patrick Donnell, and eighteen pounds to be paid George Ormsby, Esq, for transporting Edmond Connolly, John Roe and Dom. Hogan.

Summer assizes 1738, twelve pounds paid to John Blakeney, Esq, for transporting Connor Lynne.

Summer assizes 1740, six pounds paid George Warburton, Esq, for transporting Mary Coggerill.

Summer assizes 1742, one hundred twenty-six pounds paid to Robert Pierce, Esq, for transporting Thomas Donoghoe, Patrick Bourke, Anthony St Leger, John Cahan, Richard Walsh, Patrick Dermody, Murtagh Dermody, Michael Keighry, John Daly, Augustine McCarra, Thady Martin, John Moran, John Shaughnessy, Thomas Flaherty, Hugh Dunn, Thomas Lenaghan, Murtogh Mooney, Catherine Henaghan, Patrick Kenny and Richard Lawless.

Lent assizes 1738, twenty pounds paid to John Blakeney, Esq, High-sheriff, for transporting William Bourke, John Kelly, Mary Lavendar and Honora Quane.

Lent assizes 1738, eighteen pounds presented and paid to Richard Trench, Esq, for transporting Thady Lally and Connor Lyons.

COUNTY OF THE TOWN OF GALWAY

Sumer assizes 1743, ten pounds raised and paid to the Mayor for transporting Thomas White and William Burn.

COUNTY OF LEITRIM

Summer assizes 1736, twenty-four pounds presented for transporting James Sunnaghan, Thomas and Bryan McSharry.

Summer assizes 1742, the sum of forty-eight pounds raised and paid to Booth Gore, Esq, High-sheriff for transporting Bryan Kelly, Martin Mulloy, Bryan McWeeny, Francis Morrison, William Wilson, Patrick McGlinn, Mable McCarty and Luke Neilan.

COUNTY OF MAYO

Summer assizes, 1736, twenty pounds presented to be paid Mitchelburn Knox merchant, being so much remained due to him for transporting seven vagabonds and convicts that had been sent to be transported, and twenty-five pounds sterling, presented summer assizes 1738, for the maintainance of ten convicts and vagabonds that had been sent to Sligoe.

COUNTY OF SLIGOE

Lent assizes 1736, sixty-six pounds presented and paid to James Sodon, Esq, for transporting John Cullen, James Sharcot, John Kenny, John Hussey, Neil McHugh, James Fitzmorris, Thomas Forragher, Patrick Forragher, Bridget Costelloe and Catherine McGlinn.

Summer assizes 1740, eighteen pounds presented to be paid Charles o'Hara, Esq for transporting John Farrell, otherwise Trawly, otherwise Fitzgerald, Michael Connolly and Thady Kegan, and lent Assixes 1739, twenty-four pounds presented to be paid Blashford Hughs, Esq, for transporting Dennis Higgins, Bridget Harcan, Henry Bram and Joan Gawny.

Summer assizes 1741, six pounds to be paid Christopher Duke, Sub-sheriff for transporting John Galway.

Summer assizes 1742, the sum of thrity-six pounds to be paid to John Percival, Esq for transporting Daniel Mullican, Teigue McMoroy, Patrick Jordan, William Bourke, Dennis Kilmartin and John Mealy otherwise Johnins.

COUNTY OF ROSCOMMON

Lent assizes 1736, the sum of six pounds presented to be paid John Harward, Esq, for transporting James Gaynor.

Summer assizes 1737, nine pounds four shillings and six pence paid to Usher St.George, Esq, for transmitting and transporting Michael Kenney.

Lent assizes 1738, five pounds paid Bartholomew Mahon, Esq, for transporting Bryan Monaghan.

Lent assizes 1739, five pounds paid to Thomas Lyster, Esq, for transporting Bryan Mirachane, and five pounds for transporting Laughlin Naghten.

Summer assizes 1739, twelve pounds to be paid to Thomas Lyster, Esq, for transporting Garret Coghy and Bryan Monaghan.

Summer assizes 1740, six pounds to be paid Henry St. George, Esq, for transporting Thady Lyons.

Summer assizes 1741, five pounds to be paid to Thomas Mahon, Esq, for transporting Bryan Coyne.

Lent assizes 1742, fifteen pounds in the hands of Dr Manley to be paid Gilbert King, Esq, for transporting three criminals.

Summer assizes 1741, five pounds to be paid the same for transporting Patrick Flannegan.

I humbly certify the foregoing list to be a true list of the several persons who were ordered for transportation as felons and vagabonds, tried and presented at the several assizes held in and for the foregoing Counties in the Province of Connaught, from Summer assizes 1735 to and for Summer assizes 1743, inclusive, and that the several grand juries of the several Counties aforesaid, presented the several sums herein before mentioned for the transportation of the several persons for which the said money is mentioned to be raised and paid, amounting in the whole to the sum of five hundred and forty-nine pounds four shillings and six pence, and don't find that there was any other sum or sums of money presented by the grand juries of the said several Counties or any of them, for transporting of any of the other persons in this list contained during the said time.   Dated this sixteenth day of January 1743.
    William Knox, Clerk of the Crown for the province of Connaught.

COUNTY OF CLARE

A list of all the convicted felons and vagabonds who have been ordered for transportation for these seven years last past, with an account of what money hath been raised for those purposes in the said County of Clare, returned by Richard England, Clerk of the Crown of the said County, pursuant to an order of the honourable House of Commons in Ireland, bearing date the tenth of December 1743.

Summer assizes 1736

Barnaby Reilly	Transported as felons and a presentment	
John Collins	made in favour of John Brady, Esq then	
William Ryan	Sheriff for transporting them of	£ 18

Lent assizes 1737

Barnaby Burns	Transported as a felon, and presentment made in favour of St John Bridgeman, Esq, then Sheriff of the said County for transporting him of	£ 18

Summer assizes 1741

Matthias Touhy	Transported as felons, and a presentment	
Charles Hehir	made in favour of John Stackpole, Esq,	
Michael Hynes	then Sheriff of the said County for	
Honora Neale	transporting them of	£ 48
Darby Kean		
William Riedy		
Martin o'Mara		
John Riedy		

Summer assizes 1742

Michael Hynes	Ordered for transportation as felons, and a	
John McNamara	presentment made in favour of Robert	
Martin Mears	Harrison, Esq, then Sheriff of said County,	
John Riedy	for transmitting them to Limerick and fees	
William Riedy	paid by him for transporting them of	£ 42
Darby Kean		
Thomas McGrath		
William Curtane		
David Doyle		
John Baghane		
Patrick McNamara		
Michael Fahy		
Honora Forave		
Mary McGrath		
John Bevlan		

Lent assizes 1743.

James Kean   Ordered for transportation, and a presentment
Andrew Ryan   made in favour of James Butler, Esq, Sheriff
Michael Cloon   of the said County, for transmitting and
transporting them of   £ 24

Total   £138

Examined by Richard England, Clerk of the Crown.

An account of money paid by John King treasurer of the County of Dublin
and his Predecessor, and to whom, for these seven years last past, for the
transportation of felons and vagabonds, presented by the several grand
juries of the county of Dublin and his Majesty's Court of King's Bench.

		£
Easter term 1738	To Mr William Scriven Under-Sheriff	12
Michaelmas term 1738	To the same	36
Hillary term 1739	To Mr John Cooke Under-Sheriff	30
Trinity term 1741	To Mr Redmond Kane Under-Sheriff	50
Michaelmas term 1741	To the same	50
Hillary term 1741	To the same	75
Trinity term 1743	To Mr Richard Rickison Under-Sheriff	15
	Total	268

I humbly certify that the above sums (and no more) were presented, raised
and paid by me and my predecessor to the several persons above
mentioned, at his Majesty's court of King's Bench, for these seven years
last past, for the transportation of felons and vagabonds.   Dated this first
day of February 1743.

John King, treasurer of the County of Dublin.

An account of what money has been raised at the general quarter sessions of the peace held for the County of Dublin for transporting of felons and vagabonds for these seven years last past.

£

July Sessions 1737
For transporting John Moore, Ann Jones, Mary Butterfield, Mary Dowling and Mary Hobbs, there was raised by presentment and paid to Thomas Granger, Esq, then High-Sheriff the sum of   30

October Sessions 1737
For transporting of Thomas Cahill, Laughlin Bergin, William Baning, Joseph McCormick and Ann Conolly there was raised by presentment and paid to Terence Kerin then Under-Sheriff the sum of   15

April Sessions 1738.
For transporting Thomas Thelony, James Fitzpatrick Arthur McMullen, Thomas Tallant, Patrick Dempsey, Daniel Giraghty, John Reilly and Daniel Fox convicted at the commission of Oyer and Terminer, there was raised by presentment and paid to Richard Rickison then Under-Sheriff the sum of   40

October Sessions 1738
For transporting Thady Gray and Ralph Venables, both convicted at the said commission, there was raised by presentment and paid to William Scrivens then Under-Sheriff the sum of   12

May Sessions 1739
For transporting of Faughney Farrell and Patrick Sheridan, both convicted at said commission, there was raised by presentment and paid to said William Scriven the sum of   12

July Sessions 1739
For transporting John Reilly and Patrick Dowling, both convicted at said commission, and for transmitting of prisoners, and for the expense that John Cooke then Under-Sheriff was at in attending the execution of John Flanagan and others with guards, there was raised by presentment and paid to said Cooke the sum of twenty pounds; and as it does not appear what part of said sum was raised for transporting the said Reilly and Dowling, I have returned the full sum raised as aforesaid.   20

Cont'd

85

October Sessions 1740
For transporting Daniel Clayton, David Hendrick and Thomas
Scarffe, there was raised by presentment and paid to Robert
Robinet then Under-Sheriff of said County, the sum of   18

April Sessions 1743
For transporting Daniel Wolaghan, Darby Hanlan, John Power,
Edward Cawlan, Elizabeth Ryan, John McGuire, Hester McGuire,
James McGuire and Peter Bath, convicted at said Sessions and at
the commission of Oyer and Terminer, there was raised by present-
ment and paid to the then Sheriff the sum of   45

October Sessions 1742
For transporting of Thomas Murphy, Catherine Byrne, Judith
Freeman otherwise Byrn, Mary Anderson, Bridget Mealy, Catherine
Wall, James Laughlin, Felix Doyle and John Ryan, convicted at
said Sessions and said commission, there was raised by present-
ment and paid to the then Sheriff the sum of   45

January Sessions 1742
For transporting William Flyn otherwise Leathercap, David Lawler
and Thomas Moran, convicted at said Sessions, there was raised by
presentment and paid to the then Sheriff the sum of   15
                                                        Total   62

Thomas Greene, Dep. Clk. Peace County Dublin

An account of what money has been raised on the County of Dublin at the
Quarter-Sessions, and to whom paid by John King treasurer of said County
and his predecessor for these seven years last past, for the transportation
of felons and vagabonds.

		£
July Sessions 1737	To Thomas Granger, Esq; High Sheriff	30
October Sessions 1737	To Mr Terence Kerin Under-Sheriff	25
April Sessions 1738	To Mr Richard Rickison Under-Sheriff	40
October Sessions 1738	To Mr William Scriven Under-Sheriff	12
May Sessions 1739	To the same	12
July Sessions 1739	To Mr John Cook Under-Sheriff	10
October Sessions 1740	To Mr Robert Robinet Under-Sheriff	18
April Sessions 1742	To Mark Synnot, Esq; High-Sheriff	45
October Sessions 1742	To the same	45
January Sessions 1740	To the same	15
April Sessions 1743	To the same	15
	Total	267

I humbly certify that the above sums (and no more) were raised at the quarter-sessions of the County of Dublin, and paid by me and my predecessor to the several persons above mentioned, within these seven years last past, for the transportation of felons and vagabonds. Dated this first day of February 1743.

John King, Treasurer of the County of Dublin

A list of the prisoners that died in the goal of Newgate since the year 1737.

25 July 1738
Patrick McKay, Elizabeth Slater

17 January 1739
James Bryan

10 April 1739
Philip Magennis

26 May 1739
John Byrn

3 June 1739
Thomas Quin

6 October 1739
Patrick Finn

1 October 1740
John Roberts

21 December 1740
Rose Ash

7 January 1740
Judith Lamb

18 January 1740
Patrick Duffy

26 January 1740
Henry Keating

Cont'd

87

14 February 1740
   Matthew Maher

17 February 1740
   Ann Bray

24 February 1740
   Thomas Elmes

28 February 1740
   David Anderson

7 March 1740
   Morgan Redmond

10 March 1740
   Thomas Scarfe

3 April 1741
   Bartholomew Hoare

24 April 1741
   William Murphy

27 April 1741
   Morgan Byrn

17 May 1741
   Patrick Meaghan, Patrick Flinn

19 June 1741
   John Ferguson

3 July 1741
   Patrick Gronty, Mary Byrn

1742
   Mary Ryan, Jane Ryan, Elinor Joice

1743
   John Underwood

The above is a true list, this second of February 1743.

Thomas Smith

A list of transports shipped off from the year 1735 to the first of
February 1743-4.

4 Feb 1735	Delivered thirty to Isaac Kelsick on board the Union
3 ditto 1735-6	Delivered twenty-three to Ja. Stevenson on board the Bruce
12 ditto	Delivered to ditto two
23 Mar	Deivered three to Thomas Manning
18 Feb 1736	Delivered to Isaac Kelsick twenty-eight
30 Mar ditto	Delivered to James Byrn one
4 Apr	Delivered to Morgan Farrell fourteen
20 May	Delivered to James Stevenson two
11 Mar	Delivered to Richard Ribson twelve
13 Jul	Delivered to George Gibson seven
14 May	Delivered to James Stevenson four
17 Aug	Delivered to Christopher Quinn one
22 Feb 1737	Delivered to John Martin thirty-three
23 May	Delivered to James Stevenson nineteen on board the Dublin Merchant
30 ditto	Delivered to ditto on board ditto one
26 ditto	Delivered to Daniel Magill fourteen on board ditto
19 Aug	Delivered to Tho Seabrooke ten on board the brig Orange
23 Feb 1737-8	Delivered to William Fisher two
12 Apr 1738	Delivered to Alexander Montgomery three
24 ditto	Delivered to Peter Cullen four
28 ditto	Delivered to James Patten three
6 May	Delivered to ditto five on board the Walpole
15 May	Delivered to Robet Harper on board the Walpole seven
30 Aug	Delivered to John Hornby seventeen
13 Nov	Delivered to Isaac Kelsick twenty-five
5 Dec	Delivered to James Bonnet one on board the Virgin-Queen
24 Mar 1739	Deliverd to John Maylor six on board the snow Flower-Deluce
24 Jan	Delivered to Sam Oliver on board the Antigua packet twenty
18 Apr	Delivered to John Wright on board the Rachael of Saltcoats twenty-six
27 May	Delivered to Thomas Steel on board the Southwell three
3 Jun	Delivered to ditto on board of ditto eleven
26 Jun 1739	Delivered to Pat. Horish on board the Cartbagena six
4 Mar 1740	Delivered to Nathaniel Scars twenty-three
14 Jul	Delivered to Pat. Roe five on board the Three Friends
30 Jun 1741	Delivered to Edward Hagan eight.
29 ditto	Delivered to ditto on board the Two Friends six
Cont'd	

6 Jul	Delivered to ditto eleven
12 Aug	Delivered to Jacob Willard on board the <u>St Andrew Maryland</u> two
21 Sep	Delivered to William Codd on board the <u>Southwell</u> fifty-five
8 Feb	Delivered to Elisha Johnson on board the <u>William of Rhode-Island</u> fifty-two
8 Jul	Delivered to Mark Talbot on board the <u>Two Friends of Dublin</u> six
11 Aug	Delivered to --- on board the brigantine <u>St Audone</u> ten
23 Mar	Delivered to Richard Goodman twenty-two
6 May 1740	Delivered to John Dyatt eleven on board the <u>Batchelor of Dublin</u>
5 Sep	Delivered to Andrew Buckler on board the <u>Baltimore</u> brigantine twenty-two
2 Jul 1741	Delivered to Edward Hagan fourteen
22 Mar 1742	Delivered to Tim Donovan on board the <u>Whitehaven</u> Galley twenty-six
28 ditto	Delivered to William Jackson on board ditto four
26 Aug	Delivered to William Basnot on board of the <u>Santry</u> seventy-eight
29 Sep	Delivered to James Campbell on board the <u>Molly of Whitehaven</u> Galley sixty-three
5 Oct	Delivered to James Campbell eighteen
21 Apr 1743	Delivered to John Martin on board the <u>George of Dublin</u> forty-five
21 May	Delivered to William Postlethwaite seven
20 Aug	Delivered to Benjamin Bourke eighteen
9 Nov	Delivered to Robert Harper on board the <u>Charming Peggy</u> one
18 Jun	Delivered to Joseph Tyrrell on board the <u>Richard of Dublin</u> one
28 Jul 1738	Delivered to Richard Durham two
14 Apr ditto	Delivered to Thomas Robinson two
15 ditto	Delivered to ditto one

Thomas Smyth

In obedience to the commands of the honourable Committee appointed to inspect the returns of felons and vagabonds ordered for transportation.

John Hornby most humbly presents to your honours a list of all the felons and vagabonds, by him contracted for and shipped off these seven years last past, so far as he can possibly collect by his books and memory, viz.

90

Constant McDaniel
John Savage
James Bermingham
John Quinlan
Ralph Venables
Peter Cannon
Elenor Kelly
Thady Gray

Mary Christian
Saragh Dungan
Laughlin Murphy
John Campbell
Doroty Ryan
Thady Flanagan
Patrick Connor

The above fifteen persons indented the twenty-ninth of August 1738, for seven years, for which the said Hornby has received from Mr Alexander Carroll the City Treasurer the sum of thirty-nine pounds for transporting the same on board the Appleby for Virginia, where they were accordingly landed, but no certificate returned for any of them, the merchant not having directions to apply for such certificates, as said Hornby had no manner of intimation that the same were necessary, otherwise could easily have obtained them.   Dublin, second of February 1743.

John Hornby

A list of twenty-two convicts transported on board the Hibernia, Nathaniel Sears, master, for Maryland in March 1740, by Thomas Cooke merchant, the second of February 1743.

Thomas Cooke

Thomas Finn
John Bourke
Walter Shean
James Donovan
Mary Halfpenny
Dennis Clayton
Philip Williams
Lucy Coleman
James McCawley
Dennis Dunn
Henry Bryan

John Hill
Ann Nugent
Elizabeth Long
Peter Cochlan
Patrick Reilly
Catherine Reilly
Christopher Hicky
John Layer
James Walsh
Thomas Paterson
Patrick Cowlan

At three pounds each.

A return of sales of twenty servants from on board the ship, Hibernia
Nathaniel Sears, master, for account of Mr Thomas Cooke merchant in
Dublin.

Servants Names	To whom sold	L	s	d
Thomas Finn	Nicholas George for cash	13	10	0
Ann Nugent	Nicholas Hyland	11	10	0
James Donovan	Peter Boyer	13	10	0
Patrick Reilly				
Philip Ze Williams				
John Layer				
Dennis Dunn				
Henry Bryan				
John Hill				
Walter Shean				
Peter Cochlan				
Dennis Clayton				
Christopher Hicky				
James McCowley				
Thomas Paterson				
Patrick Cowlan				
John Bourk				
Elizabeth Long				
Mary Halfpenny				
Catherine Reilly	Robert Alison at £9.10s each	161	10	0
Lucy Coleman	Sold by Daniel Dulanse, Esq			
James Walsh	Maryland			

Total   200 00   00
Philadelphia, 25 February 1741
Davey and Carsan

In the ship, Sentry of Dublin, William Basnet commander, were imported
the following convicts.

Mary Howard	Bridget Clark
John Ryan	Judith Freeman
Mary Hutchinson	John McHar
Mary Burn	Mary Martin
John Reynolds	Elenor Hutchinson
Catherine Wael	James Lyon
Margaret Hored	Bridget Mealy
James Quin	Catherine Johnson
Cont'd	

Patrick Kenny
Patrick Carpenter
Thomas Nudham
Susannah Bourk
Mary Roach
Roger Sweeney
Dennis Doyle
Catherine Doyle
James Newman
Patrick Kinshella
Mary Maguire
John Jones
Thomas Lynch
Margaret Cary
Thomas Goodman
Thomas Roony
Mary Stone
Terence Murphy
John Sherlock
Andrew Kewing
George Osburn
Edward Toole
John Condrum
Bryan Doran
Terence Reilly
Thomas Murphy
William Lynch
John Bannam
Henry Fitzwilliams

Walter Murphy
Margaret Johnson
Christopher Smith
Peter Fitzpatrick
John Nowland
Eleanor Burrows
John Clark
Nicholas Furlon
Jane Ball
Robert Bryan
Laughlin Curry
Alice Ulster
Edward Ivory
Darby Kelly
Sarah Donelly
Lewis Murphy
John Roony
William Dulany
Richard Kenim
Michael Hagall
Feelix Doyle
John Doyle
Joseph Erwin
William Desbrit
John Kelly
Thomas Fleming
Roger Carney
Patrick Grace

Port Anapolis in Maryland
These are to certify that the above persons were here imported as
aforesaid the fifth day of November 1742; and that the same persons
being called over, did severally answer to their names. Given under my
hand and seal this tenth day January in the seventeenth year of the reign
of our sovereign Lord King George the Second, King of Great-Britain,
France and Ireland, etc, Annoq. Dom. 1742:

Benjamin Tasker, naval officer.

An account of what money was received by Redmond Kane for transporting
felons and vagabonds, with a list of such felons and vagabonds for seven
years last past, and the names of the merchants by whom they were
transported.

93

	L
Trinity 1741, received	50
Michaelmas 1741, received	50
Hilary 1741, received	75
Total	175

The Persons Transported

Trinity 1741
William Murphy, John Hill, Edward Graham, John Geogarty, John Redmond, Bryan McAtire, James Walsh, Thomas Hoey, John Dorman, Francis Neal.

Michaelmas 1741
Mary Maguire, Mary Lawler, John Howard, Edward Wilson, William Shortley, Catherine Delany, Owen Murphy, Thomas Ryder, Hugh Reily, Mary Cologan.

Hilary 1741
Peter Reilly, Teresa Dignam, Elizabeth Hyland, Thomas Kearnan, Patrick Kilkelly, Patrick Johnson, Matthew Tearnan, Sarah Ryan, John Gagarty, William Cane, Walter Hughs, Rachel Everston, John Carroll, John Farrell and George Forster.

Merchants
Mr Thomas Cooke, Mr Samuel Lyons, Mr Bird, and Mr Joseph Weld.
This is the return of Redmond Kane.

An account of all money by me received by virtue of any presentments of the grand juries of the County of Dublin for these seven years last past, for transporting any convict felons and vagabond, with the account of such convict felons and vagabonds, as also an account of what sums of money I have received by virtue of any presentments of the grand juries of the said County during the said time, as High-Sheriff, and for what purpose.

		L	s	d
April 1742	For transporting Daniel Wholaghan, Darby Hanlan, John Power, Edward Caulan, Elizabeth Ryan, John Maguire, Esther Maguire, James Maguire and Peter Bath	45	0	0
Same sessions Cont'd	For erecting a gallows at Kilmainhan	2	7	6

October 1742	For transporting Thomas Murphy, Catherine Byrn, Judith Freeman otherwise Byrn, Mary Anderson, Bridget Maley, Catherine Wall, James Laughlin Foelix Doyle and John Ryan	45	0	0
January 1742	For transporting William Flinn otherwise Leathercap, David Lawler and Thomas Moran	15	0	0
April 1743	For transporting Mary Gorman, Patrick Carroll and Daniel Hughs	15	0	0
	Total	122	7	0

Dated this fourth day of February 1743.
Mark Synnot, late High Sheriff of the County of Dublin

An account of what presentments were granted by the grand jury of the county of Dublin at the sessions of Kilmainham for transporting of felons and vagabonds since the fourteenth of July 1737, and paid to Richard Rickison the Under-Sheriff to April 1738.

L

14 Jul 1737   For transporting John Moore, Ann Jones, Mary
Butterfield, Mary Dowling and Mary Hobbs,
bound to James Stephenson Esq; put on board
the Dublin, but can't tell the master's name   30

April 1738   For transporting Thomas Tholmey, James
Fitzpatrick, Arthur McMullen, Thomas Tallant,
Patrick Dempsey, Daniel Girraghty, John Reilly
and Daniel Fox, Captain Martin merchant, but
can't tell the mast or ship's name   40

An account of what felons and vagabonds were transported from the commission of Oyer and Terminer for the county of dublin, for the year 1743 by Richard Rickison Under-Sheriff, and presented by the grand jury.

Trinity 1743   For transporting Daniel Dolan, Patrick Byrne
and James Delany, Charles Weld merchant, put on
board the George of Dublin, but can't tell the
master's name   15

October 1743   For transporting Patrick Purcell and Joan Barefoot
from the commission in the ship of Charming Peggy
John Cossart marchant, Robert Harper master, the
money presented but not raised by the County   10

Signed   Richard Rickison   Total   95

95

A list of prisoners that died in Newgate from the eighth day of October 1737, to the first day of February 1743

25 Jul 1738
   Patrick McKay

17 Jan 1738
   James Bryan

10 Apr 1739
   Philip Magennis

26 May 1739
   John Byrn

3 Jun 1739
   Thomas Quin

6 Oct 1739
   Patrick Finn

18 Jan 1740
   Patrick Duffey

26 Jan 1740
   Henry Keating

14 Feb 1740
   Matthew Maher

17 Feb 1740
   Ann Bray

24 Feb 1740
   Thomas Elmes

7 Mar 1740
   Morgan Redmond

10 Mar 1740
   Thomas Scarffe

24 Apr 1740
   William Murphy

Cont'd

27 Apr 1740
  Morgan Byrn

19 Jul 1740
  John Ferguson

3 Jul 1740
  Patrick Groudy, Mary Byrn, Mary Ryan, Jane Ryan, John Underwood

25 Jul 1742
  Elizabeth Slator

18 Sep 1742
  Elizabeth Brooks

3 Oct 1740
  John Roberts

22 Dec 1740
  Rose Ash

9 Jan 1740
  Judith Lamb

28 Feb 1740
  David Henderson to be transported

9 Feb 1741
  Neal Duffey, Jane Ryan

2 Mar 1741
  Elizabeth Long

3 Apr 1741
  Batholomew Hore

12 May 1741
  Philip Meaghan

28 May 1741
  Patrick Flynn

3 Jul 1741
  Thomas Harahane to be transported

Cont'd

3 Feb 1741
    Elenor Joyce

I have the inquisitions.
David Tew Coroner

A list of inquests held in Newgate on prisoners from May the third 1737

3 May 1737
    Mary Coffee

8 Jun 1739
    James Hananage to be transported

5 Oct 1739
    Patrick Flinn to be transported

29 Jun 1741
    Thady Fergusan

16 Jul 1741
    Mary Byrne to be transported

21 Jul 1741
    Honora McNally to be transported

21 Aug 1741
    John Mullegan to be transported

7 Sep 1741
    Michael Mara to be transported

7 Jan 1741
    Richard Page

29 Jan 1741
    Patrick Carroll

22 Feb 1741
    Mary Ryan

17 Jun 1743
    Thomas Newall
Cont'd

17 Dec 1743
John Underwood

William Walker, Coronor

Account of what money has been presented in the County of the City of Dublin for transporting convict felons and vagabonds for seven years last past, and to whom paid

		L	s	d
1737, Midsummer	To James Stephenson Esq	63	0	0
Michaelmas and	Isaac Kelsick	102	0	0
Christmas Sessions	John Martin	75	0	0
	Joseph Weld	21	0	0
1738, Easter Sessions	Thomas Robinson	3	0	0
	William Tiffin	6	0	0
	Peter Cullen	12	0	0
	Alexander Montgomery	15	0	0
Michaelmas Sessions	Richard Durham	6	0	0
1739 Midsummer	Joseph Weld	111	0	0
Sessions	Samuel Horner	3	0	0
	Isaac Kelsick	33	0	0
	Joseph Hornby	39	0	0
1740, Midsummer	Joseph Weld	45	0	0
Sessions	Samuel Lyons	60	0	0
	Thomas Steel	15	0	0
Christmas Sessions	Thomas Cooke	64	0	0
1741, Midsummer	Samuel Lyons and Oliver Bird	69	0	0
Sessions	Walter Codd	27	0	0
	Jacob Willard	27	0	0
Christmas Sessions	Joseph Weld	90	0	0
	Richard Goodman	54	0	0
1742, Midsummer,	John Langley These sums not	(96	0	0
Michaelmas and	James Campbell as yet collected	(48	0	0
Easter Sessions	John Martin	(48	0	0
		(		

Cont'd

99

1743, Midsummer,	John Langley	(21	0	0
and Michaelmas	John Langley	(6	0	0
Sessions	Robert Harper	(3	0	0

| | Total | 1161 | 0 | 0 |

4 Feb 1743
Alexander Carroll, treasurer of the publick money Co City of Dublin

An account of all sums of money that have been presented in the County of Dublin, and paid to High-Sheriffs or Sub-Sheriffs for these seven years last past, and for what particular service; over and above the particular sums presented to be paid to them for transporting felons and vagabonds.

	L	s	d

April Sessions 1737
To Mr Richard Rickison Sub-sheriff for transporting prisoners, quelling riots, for bolts for the use of the goal, and money expended on the guards in pillorying William Banning

| | 20 | 0 | 0 |

Easter term 1737
To the same for quelling a great and dangerous mobb, who for several Sundays and holydays riotously assembled on the commons of Kilmainham, and there and in other parts adjoining committed great affrays, and for apprehending, prosecuting and convicting John Berren, one of the rioters, and for his expenses in whipping Archibald Kerby and John McCormack in Swords.

| | 30 | 0 | 0 |

July Sessions 1737
To the same, for the maintenance of five persons in custody from the eleventh of March to the twenty-eighth of April, at two pence per day

| | 2 | 0 | 0 |

April Sessions 1738
To Mr William Scriven, Sub-sheriff, for quelling riots in the several parts of the County, and for bolts and shackles for the use of the goal

| | 20 | 0 | 0 |

October Sessions 1738
To the same, for transmitting prisoners, and for money laid out for the use of the County

| | 30 | 0 | 0 |

Cont'd
May Sessions 1739
To Mr John Cooke Sub-sheriff, for quelling several riots,
and for money laid out for the use of the County   30   0   0

July Sessions 1739
To the same, for transmitting prisoners, and for the
expense he was at in attending the execution of John
Flannigan, Nicholas Ball and Daniel Neal with guards   10   0   0

October Sessions 1739
To the same, for providing bolts and shackles for the
use of the goal, and for transmitting prisoners   20   0   0

January Sessions 1739
To the same, for quelling several riots on the Lord's
Day in several parts of the County, and for raising a
guard for the same   20   0   0

July Sessions 1740
To Mr Robert Robinet Sub-sheriff, for his care and
trouble in apprehending and bringing in several persons
on the process, who had not accounted for the publick
money, as also for quelling several routs and riots in
several parts of the County   20   0   0

October Sessions 1740
To the same, as a gratuity and reward for his diligent
and faithful discharge of his office in executing the
King's process against all persons, who detained the
publick money, and for his great care, trouble and
expense in preserving the publick peace   20   0   0

January Sessions 1740
To the same, as a recompence for his diligence and
expense in executing the process and bringing to
justice several high-constables and others, who
detained the publick money, and also for executing
several orders issued from the Government with
great integrity, and particularly an order of late for
inspecting and computing the corn of this County and
the species thereof, and returning a faithful account
thereof to the Government, and also for discharging
and setting at liberty great numbers of poor prisoners
without fees for one year past, being a time of great
rigour and calamity   20   0   0

Cont'd
July Sessions 1741
To Mr Redmond Kane Sub-sheriff for his great care,
expense and trouble in suppressing riots in different
parts of the County, and for apprehending and bringing
in several persons on the process, who had not
accounted for the publick money, and for transmitting
prisoners, and for discharging several poor prisoners
without fees, who were tryed for different offences
in this County   20   0   0

October Sessions 1741
To the same, for his care in suppressing riots, discharging a great number of poor prisoners without fees, and
executing the process against the high and petty
constables and other persons for the publick money   30   0   0

January Sessions 1741
To the same, for his trouble and expenses in prosecuting
convicting and executing several murderers at the
commission of Oyer and Terminer, and for exonerating
several inhabitants of the County of fines payable by
them on the green wax process, and for discharging a
great number of prisoners without fees   20   0   0

April Sessions 1742
To Mark Synnot, Esq, High-sheriff, for erecting a gallows 2   7   6

April Sessions 1743
To Mr Richard Rickison, Sub-sheriff, for his great service
and expense in quelling several mobbs and riots in several
parts of the County   50   0   0

Easter term 1743
To the same, for his expenses in erecting a pillory in
New-market and pillorying Robert Brady, he having
several men in arms to suppress the mobb, and for
whipping John Bourke, William Hoey, Edmond Dogherty,
and Mary Carrick in several parts of the County   20   0   0

July Sessions 1743
To the same, for money by him expended in repairing
the chairs and tables in the Justices and Judges rooms,
and for iron work and other services by him done for
the use of the County   22   15   0
Cont'd

October Sessions 1743
To the same, for his good attendance in suppressing
riots and mobbs in the County of Dublin, and especially
at the commons of Kilmainham and Bolphin's-barn, and
having men in arms, and endangering his life in doing
the same   30   0   0

January Sessions 1743
To the same, for his trouble and expenses in executing
Hugh Condron, and for whipping several prisoners who
were tryed in said County, and for slating the Session-
house, Judges room and the whole goal, and all other
necessaries that were wanting in said goal   50   0   0

Michaelmas term 1743
To the same, for his extraordinary expense and trouble
in pulling down the booths and tents on Gallows-Hill
and Stoney Batter, and suppressing the riots at said
places   10   0   0
                                                                 _____
The two last sums now collecting,   497   2   6
dated 4 February 1743
                    John King, Treasurer of the County of Dublin

An account of what money I received by presentment of the grand juries of
the County of Dublin for transporting felons and other services.

                                                                  L
Trinity term 1739
For transporting John Reilly and Patrick Dowling   10

Hilary term
For transporting Philip Magennis, John Reilly, Patrick
Dowling, Mary Lawless and Hugh Glascoe   30

May sessions
For quelling several riots, and for money laid out for
the use of the County   30

July sessions
For transporting of prisoners, for the expenses I was
at attending the execution of John Flanigan, Nicholas
Ball and Daniel Neal with guards   10

103

Cont'd
October sessions
For providing bolts and shackles for the use of the goal
and for transmitting prisoners   20

January sessions
For quelling several riots on the Lord's day in several
parts of the County, and for raising a guard for the
same   20
                                                                 --

                                        Total   120

                                                   John Cooke

A list of felons and vagabonds shipped on board the Revolution, John
Wright commander, bound from Dublin to Delaware bay in America,
September 1743.

                                                        L   s
From TRIM
John Cardiffe
Patrick Maguire
Henry Finnigan

From MULLINGAR
Philip Magawley
James Gordon   For the transporting received by
John Grivey   Sam Bathos   12   0
From CARLOW
Edmond Cavenagh   For the transporting received   3   0

From WICKLOW
Joan McNemara   For the transporting received   2   10

From the CITY OF DUBLIN
Margaret Dillon   For the transporting received a
Mary Drury   presentment for six pounds, no
                      part of which has been yet paid

                                                   John Langley

A list of felons and vagabonds shipped on board the <u>Sarah</u>, Richard Berrell commander, bound from Dublin to Delaware by in America, August 1743.

		L	s
From the COUNTY OF WICKLOW			
Michael Doyle			
Elizabeth Dunn			
Margaret Nowland			
als. Margaret Lennon	For the transporting received	7	1 0
From the QUEEN'S COUNTY			
Dennis Ryan			
Joan Butler			
Patrick Moore			
Roger Gormill	For the transporting received	1 0	0
From the COUNTY OF CAVAN			
Isaac Burn			
Arthur Burn	For the transporting received	5	0
From the KING'S COUNTY			
Laurence Hand	For the transporting received	3	0
From the COUNTY OF LONGFORD			
Henry Hyland	For the transporting received		
From the CITY OF DUBLIN			
Laurence Langen			
Catherine Burn			
Dominick Hogan			
Winifred Linton	For the transporting received		
William Kennedy	a presentment for twenty-one		
Patrick Smith	pounds, no part of which has		
Edward Dogherty	yet been paid		

John Langley

A list of felons and vagabonds shipped on board the <u>Santry</u>, William Bassnet commander, bound from Dublin to Maryland in America, in 1742.
by John Langley & Co

		L	s	d
From the COUNTY OF CARLOW				
Thomas Fleming				
Bryan Doran				
William Linchy				
Edmond Evory				
John Kealy				
Dennis Doyle				
Peter Fitzpatrick				
Edmond Toole				
John Nowland				
Terence Reily	For the transporting received	27	9	11
From WICKLOW				
Henry Fitzwilliams				
John Doyle				
Terence Murphy				
Loughlin Keary				
John Reynolds				
Sarah Donelly				
George Ashburn				
Walter Murphy				
Lewis Murphy				
Richard Kerivan	For the transporting received	30	0	0
From the QUEEN'S COUNTY				
John Couran				
als Donald				
William Donald				
als Despard				
Patrick Grace				
Michael Hogan				
Roger Carney				
William Delany				
Thomas Goodwin				
Darby Kelly				
John Sherlock	For the transporting received	27	0	0
From the COUNTY OF KILDARE				
Patrick Kinshelagh				
Mary Burne				
Owen Slattery	For the transporting received	9	0	0

Cont'd
From the COUNTY OF LONGFORD
Thomas Needham
Patrick Kenny   For the transporting received   2   0   0

From the COUNTY OF DUBLIN
John Ryan
Feelix Doyle
James Loughlin
Catherine Wale
Bridget Maley
Mary Anderson
Judith Freeman
Catherine Burn
Thomas Murphy   For the transporting received   27   0   0

From the CITY OF DUBLIN
John Magher
John Jones
James Newham
Nicholas Furlong
Christopher Smith
Jane Ball
Bridget Clark
Mary Haydon
Alice Tresom
Mary Hutchison
Elinor Hutchison
Mary Maguire
Catherine Johnson
Margaret Johnson
Mary Roache
Ann Keary
Margaret Hand
Mary Martin
Patrick Carpenter
Thomas Rooney
John Rooney
James Lynagh
Mary Stoner
Susanna Burke
Catherine Doyle
Andrew Kerewine   For the transporting these and
John Bannon   the following three, received a
John Clark   presentment for ninety-six
Roger Sweeney   pounds, no part of which is yet

```
                          paid                          96    0    0
Ellenor  Burrows)
James Quin        )       Landing,  for  which  certificate
Robert o'Brien    )           is  returned

                                              John Langley
```

Upon the whole, your Committee beg leave to observe, that as these returns from the several Clerks of the Crown in this kingdom, were moved for on the tenth day of November last past, and that the last of these returns were not brought in and laid before the House till the first day of this instant February, they have not had it in their power, (from the shortness of time) to prosecute this inquiry in the manner the nature thereof merited and required, whereby many and great frauds and abuses of the laws now in force, for transporting of convict felons and vagabonds, might have properly been detected and made known to the publick, nevertheless upon what has appeared to the committee relative to the County of the City of Dublin and County of Dublin, in the progress of their enquiry and inspection of said returns, the Committee on re-considering their said report, came to the following resolutions.

Resolved, that it appears to this Committee by the returns made to the House, that the number of convict felons and vagabonds, ordered for transportation these seven years last past, amounts to one thousand nine hundred and twenty persons.

Resolved, that it appears to this Committee by the returns made to the House, that the sum of eight thousand four hundred and twenty-eight pounds five shillings and five-pence sterling hath been presented and raised off the several Counties in this kingdom these seven years last past, for transporting convict felons and vagabonds.

Ordered, that the said report, be printed; and that Mr Speaker do appoint the printing thereof, and that no person, but such as he shall apoint, to presume to print the same.

INDEX OF NAMES

Bourk, Rowland	31	Brenan, John	51
Bourke, Barbara	45, 46	Brennan, Dennis	30
Bourke, Bartholomew	49, 50	Brien, Catherine	52
Bourke, Edmond	57	Brien, Dennis	58
Bourke, Edmund	58	Brien, Henry	15
Bourke, James	29, 56	Brien, John	15
Bourke, John	15, 42,	Brien, Margaret	57
	60, 91,	Brien, Stephen	58
	92	Bright, Matthew	40
Bourke, Margaret	49	Brislane, Morgan	79
Bourke, Martin	8	Broder, Michael	57
Bourke, Mary	27	Broder, Patrick	32
Bourke, Michael	79	Broderick, John	31
Bourke, Patrick	35, 78,	Broderick, Michael	57
	80	Brogan, Patrick	38
Bourke, Susanna	16	Bromebane, John	56
Bourke, Susannah	93	Brooks, Elizabeth	97
Bourke, Theobald	27	Brosnehane, Hugh	56
Bourke, Thomas	27	Brown, David	64
Bourke, William	78, 80,	Brown, John	16, 58
	79, 81	Browne, Elizabeth	16
Bowen, Peter	37	Browne, Joan	45, 46
Bowles, Henry	32	Bruce, William	66
Boy, John	77	Bruen, Henry	79, 91
Boyd, John	69		92
Boyle, John	47, 66	Bryan, Daniel	42
Boyle, Owen	24	Bryan, Edmond	32
Boyne, Edmond	35	Bryan, James	49, 50
Brack, John	30		87, 96
Brack, Thomas	30	Bryan, John	13, 39
Bradford, Graham	11		47, 49,
Brady, Daniel	16		56
Brady, Hugh	13	Bryan, Margaret	48, 49
Brady, Judith	17		57
Brady, Margaret	71	Bryan, Mary	12, 40
Brady, Robert	11		41
Bram, Henry	81	Bryan, Miles	14
Brattan, Mary	63	Bryan, Patrick	8
Bray, Ann	15, 88,	Bryan, Richard	14
	96	Bryan, Robert	8, 93
Bray, John	25	Bryan, Sarah	10
Bray, Patrick	23	Bryan, Stumphy	68
Breene, Daniel	56	Bryan, Teigue	57

Bryan, Thomas	56	Byrne, Catherine	18, 22
Bryen, Dennis	42		86
Bryen, Teigue	40	Byrne, Charles	35
Brooks, Elizabeth	97	Byrne, Dudley	11
Buchilly, Catherine	41	Byrne, Isaac	70
Buohilly, Daniel	56	Byrne, James	35
Burk, Thomas	17	Byrne, Judith	22
Burke, William	12	Byrne, Mary	8, 14
Burn, Arthur	105		18, 22
Burn, Catherine	105, 107		30
Burn, Isaac	105	Byrne, Morgan	35
Burn, Mary	92	Byrne, Patrick	45, 95
Burn, William	80	Byrne, Owen	22
Burne, William	78	Byrne, Terence	35
Burns, Barnaby	83		
Burns, Catherine	73		
Burns, Mary	65		
Burns, Michael	68	C	
Burrows, Eleanor	93	Caffoe, Connor	53
Burrows, Ellenor	108	Caffry, Catherine	24
Bush, Margaret	48	Caffry, John	15
Butler, Catherine	14	Caghy, Garret	79
Butler, James	31	Cahane, Ellenor	43
Butler, Joan	29, 105	Cahane, Honor	59
Butler, Mary	69	Cahill, Thomas	11, 85
Butler, Pierce	31, 41	Cairney, Phelemy	74
Butler, Tobias	17	Caldwell, William	74
Butler, Walter	31	Callaghan, Cornelius	53, 63
Butler, William	17	Callaghan, Daniel	56
Butterfield, Mary	11, 85,	Callaghan, David	52
	95	Callaghan, John	16
Butterton, Thomas	13	Callaghan, Owen	25, 47,
Buyer, Mary	14		49
Byrn, Catherine	95	Callan, Bryan	63
Byrn, Francis	64	Calloghty, Owen	48
Byrn, John	87, 96	Cameran, Elizabeth	15
Byrn, Judith	86, 95	Campbell, Ann	67
Byrn, Mary	26, 88,	Campbell, Honour	51
	97, 98	Campbell, John	8, 91
Byrn, Morgan	88, 97	Campbell, Patrick	65
Byrn, Patrick	10, 46,	Cane, William	94
	58	Canlon, John	23
Byrn, Thomas	26	Cannon, Peter	8, 91

Cantillon, Thomas	11	Carthy, Timothy	32, 39
Cantwell, James	28	Carton, John (Yr)	24
Cardiffe, John	104	Carton, Peter	36
Careless, John	27	Carty, Dennis	40
Carew, Martin	58	Carty, William	16
Carew, Thomas	58	Cary, Margaret	93
Carey, William	75	Casey, Catherine	78
Carmety, Daniel	71	Casheen, Mary	16
Carney, Alice	8	Cassedy, Francis	37
Carney, James	8	Cassedy, John	68
Carney, John	14, 15	Cassedy, Maurice	72
Carney, Roger	29, 93, 106	Cassedy, Susan	71
		Cassoe, Philip	59
Carney, William	15	Caulan, Edward	94
Carpenter, Catherine	12	Caulan, James	23
Carpenter, Patrick	93, 107	Caulan, Patrick	15
Carr, Michael	78	Cavanagh, Edmond	30, 104
Carr, Samuel	76	Cavanagh, Honor	48
Carr, William	11	Cavanagh, James	37
Carragher, Patrick	25	Cavanagh, John	26
Carran, Thomas	68	Cavanagh, Margaret	32
Carrigan, James	57	Cavanagh, Tobias	8
Carrol, Brian	52	Cavenagh, Michael	22
Carroll, Catherine	18	Cawlan, Edward	11, 86
Carroll, Elizabeth	47, 49	Cawlan, Thomas Roe	25
Carroll, James	23	Cempsey, Patrick	11
Carroll, Jane	44	Chambers, Laurence	16
Carroll, John	10, 94	Champion, Thady	29
Carroll, Mary	12	Charlton, Edward	51(2)
Carroll, Patrick	11, 16, 95, 98	Cherry, Patrick	76
		Christian, Mary	13, 91
Carroll, Richard	32	Clancey, Mary	71
Carroll, Thomas	14, 23	Clancy, Mary	14
Carroll, Timothy	42	Clark, Bridget	16, 107
Carrick, Bryan	44	Clark, John	8, 63 93, 107
Carthy, Ann	13		
Carthy, Charles	49, 50	Clark, Thady	30
Carthy, Daniel	58	Clarke, Bridget	49, 50
Carthy, Florence	47, 49	Clayton, Daniel	15, 86
Carthy, Joan	55	Clayton, Dennis	91, 92
Carthy, Joanna	39	Cleary, Andrew	8
Carthy, Mary	32	Cleary, Darby	44
Carthy, Thomas	32	Cleary, Martin	58

Corban, Thomas	59	Crowly, Susanna	45
Corbet, Philip	14	Culane, Daniel	40
Corkeran, Philip	50	Cullane, Maurice	56
Corkran, Patrick	31	Cullen, Fennal	63
Cormack, Bartholomew	27	Cullen, George	35
Corran, James	30	Cullen, James	9
Corran, Michael	30	Cullen, John	81
Coser, David	79	Cullin, Fergal	75
Coskry, Michael	42	Cullitagh, Dennis	39
Coskry, Timothy	42	Cullnagh, Thomas	78
Cosly, Patrick	79	Culloghty, Owen	49
Cossee, Honora	12	Cullue, Patrick	60
Costello, Bridget	81	Cummin, Edmond	57
Costello, Charles	78	Cummin, Patrick	70
Costello, Edmund	60	Cunningham, Michael	23
Costelloe, Ann	8	Currane, John	54
Cough, John	54	Currin, Thady	31
Coughlan, Cornelius	39	Curry, Laughlin	93
Couran, John	106	Curtane, William	84
Courcey, James	52	Curtis, Henry	12
Cowlan, Patrick	91, 92	Curtis, Thomas	14
Cowley, Charles	55	Cushan, Patrick	28
Cox, Laughlin	9	Cussack, Robert	8
Coyne, Bryan	79, 82		
Cranally, Edmond	78		
Crawley, Daniel	57		
Crawly, John	45	D	
Creighton, Mary	7	Dahony, Dennis	46
Crimmeen, Cornelius	41	Dalton, Henry	37(2)
Crimmeen, Margaret	40	Dalton, James	78
Croan, Henry	63	Dalton, Patrick	58
Crocen, John	50	Daly, Bryan	70
Croneen, Ellenor	54	Daly, Daniel	36
Croneen, Joan	44	Daly, Darby	54
Croneen, Julian	43, 45	Daly, Dennis	78
Crosbie, John	56	Daly, Ellenor	25
Crotty, Mary	60	Daly, James	23
Crotty, Honor	39	Daly, John	78, 80
Crow, Owen	27	Daly, Neal	26
Crowley, Charles	39	Darcy, James	73
Crowley, Daniel	39	Darcy, Miles	33, 34
Crowley, Dennis	41	Dargan, Andrew	31
Crowley, Susanna	44	Darling, Patrick	14

Name	Page
Darrag, John	50
Daunt, Mary	44
Daunt, Philip (Eldr)	44
Daunt, Philip (Yr)	44
Daver, Daniel	79
Davis, John	12
Davis, Mary	58
Dawley, Catherine	52
Dawley, Ellenor	48, 49
Dawley, John	39, 49, 50
Dawly, Timothy	41
Dawson, John	70
Day, Sheela	64
Dean, Adam	67
Deashian, Timothy	47
Deerin, Thomas	31
Deering, Mary/Cath	12
Dehony, Thomas	57
Delahunty, Simon	26
Delany, Catherine	10, 94
Delany, Charles	28
Delany, Grizel	28
Delany, James	10, 95
Delany, John	31
Delany, William	29, 106
Dempsey, Patrick	85, 95
Denashian, Timothy	47
Denicon, Michael	79
Denneen, John	56
Dennis, James	64
Dennis, Joan	63
Deoghoe, John	35
Dermody, Murtogh	78, 80
Dermody, Patrick	80
Desbrit, William	93
Despard, William	106
Devereux, Thomas	34
Devin, Bryan	8
Devlin, Patrick	14
Dempsey, William	16
Dignam, Teresa	94
Dignam, Terress	10
Dillane, John	56
Dillane, David	41
Dillon, Margaret	18, 104
Dillon, Mary	7
Dinaghy, Teigue	56
Diwane, Michael	57
Divininy, Rose	7
Dixon, William	66
Dogherty, Catherine	49
Dogherty, Edward	18, 105
Dogherty, John	63, 76
Dogherty, Morgan	57
Dogherty, Neil	13
Dogherty, Rose	13
Doherty, Catherine	50
Dolan, Bridget	11
Dolan, Daniel	10, 95
Dollan, John	63
Donaghoe, Thomas	78
Donahoe, Cornelius	42
Donahoe, Timothy	42
Donald, Bryan	30
Donald, John	106
Donald, William	106
Donelly, Charles	73
Donelly, Sarah	35, 106
Donnell, Patrick	80
Donnelly, Edmond	70
Donnelly, Martha	12
Donnelly, Mason	16
Donoghoe, Cornelius	46, 47, 49, 56
Donoghoe, James	36
Donoghoe, John	43
Donoghoe, Michael	9
Donoghoe, Thomas	80
Donoghoe, Margaret	44
Donohoe, Michael	29
Donohoe, William	31
Donovan, Daniel	42, 44
Donovan, James	15, 91, 92
Donovan, Margaret	15
Donovan, Rickard	44, 45
Doogan, William	29

Doolin, Maurice	56	Duff, David	44
Doolin, Thomas	56	Duffey, Neal	97
Dooling, Darby	60	Duffey, Patrick	96
Doran, Bryan	30, 93, 106	Duffy, John	70
		Duffy, Patrick	15, 87
Doran, James	16, 31	Dulagh, Sarah	53
Doran, Patrick	69	Dulany, William	93
Doran, Phelemy	69	Dunbarr, James	75
Dorman, John	9, 94	Dungan, James	37
Dougherty, Roger	8	Dungan, Sarah	13
Dowd, Christopher	22	Dungan, Saragh	91
Dowdall, Edward	26	Dunn, Darby	59
Dowling, James	32	Dunn, Dennis	8, 91 92
Dowling, John	16		
Dowling, Mary	11, 85, 95	Dunn, Elizabeth	35, 105
		Dunn, Hugh	78, 80
Dowling, Patrick	9(2), 85, 103(2)	Dunn, Owen	26
		Dunn, Paul	29
Dowling, Thomas	16	Dunn, Peter	34
Dowling, William	8	Dunn, Richard	35
Downey, Bryan	25	Dunn, William	58
Downey, Darby	55	Dunphy, James	34
Downey, Dennis	56	Durass, Patrick	35
Downey, Philip	15	Durk, Edmond	78
Doyl, Michael	35	Dwyer, Anthony	57
Doyle, Andrew	31	Dwyer, John	50(2), 53
Doyle, Catherine	16, 93, 107	Dwyer, Patrick	31
		Dwyer, William	57
Doyle, David	83	Dyer, Thomas	44
Doyle, Dennis	30, 93, 106		
Doyle, Edmond	54		
Doyle, Feelix	93, 106	E	
Doyle, James	30, 34	Egan, John	60
Doyle, John	26, 35, 93, 106	Elliot, Robert	66
		Ellis, Edward	67
Doyle, Michael	17, 105	Ellord, William	28
Doyle, Murtagh	34	Elmes, Thomas	15, 88, 96
Driscoll, Darby	41		
Driscoll, Dennis	42	Enderson, John	15
Drury, Mary	18, 104	English, James	39
Duane, Timothy	39	English, John	58
Dudley, Matthew	23	English, Laurence	52

English, Mary	52	Field, James	14	
English, Patrick	25	Field, Joan	49	
English, Richard	16	Finally, John	7	
Ennis, Joan	11	Finlay, James	37	
Erwin, Joseph	93	Finlay, Pidgeon	16	
Erwin, William	8, 68	Finn, Patrick	14, 87	
Erwine, Andrew	63		96	
Everston, Rachel	94	Finn, Thomas	15, 91,	
Evisston, Rachel	10		92	
Evory, Edmond	106	Finnegan, Henry	23	
Eyers, Michael	45	Finnegan, John	26	
		Finnigan, Henry	104	
		Fishburn, George	27	
		Fitzgerald, Catherine	57	
F		Fitzgerald, Edmund	16	
Fahy, John	60	Fitzgerald, Francis	33	
Fahy, Michael	78, 83	Fitzgerald, James	52	
Fanly, John	79	Fitzgerald, John	28, 44,	
Farrell, Bryan	8		57, 79,	
Farrell, Darby	78		81	
Farrell, Faughney	85	Fitzgerald, Margaret	47	
Farrell, James	79	Fitzgerald, Mary	13, 17,	
Farrell, John	11, 52,		40(2)	
	78, 79,	Fitzgerald, Maurice	48, 49	
	81, 94	Fitzgerald, Philip	28	
Farrell, Mary	17	Fitzgerald, Thomas	42	
Farrell, Matthew	66	Fitzgerald, William	27, 44,	
Farrell, Patrick	30		45, 47,	
Farrell, Roger	30, 37		49	
Farrell, Thomas	12	Fitzgibbon, David	78	
Farrell, Walter	12	Fitzharris, Michael	35	
Fedigan, Patrick	25	Fitzmorris, James	81	
Fegan, Francis	69	Fitzpatrick, James	11, 85	
Fegan, Manus	65		95	
Fegan, Terence	65	Fitzpatrick, John	30, 71	
Ferguson, John	88, 97	Fitzpatrick, Peter	30, 93	
Ferguson, Thady	98	Fitzpatrick, Terence	71	
Fergusson, John	12	Fitzsimmons, Mary	17	
Fernsly, James	14	Fitzsimons, Bryan	14	
Ferrell, Bryan	13	Fitzsimons, Henry	16	
Ferrell, John	10	Fitzsimons, Philip	8	
Ferris, Owen	56	Fitzsymons, James	24	
Fever, James	34	Fitzwilliams, Henry	93, 106	

Flanagan, Bridget	74	Fraly, Thomas	52
Flanagan, James	74	Freeman, Judith	22, 86,
Flanagan, John	46, 85,		95, 107
	103	Frenighty, Daniel	56
Flanagan, Patrick	36	Furlon, Nicholas	93
Flanagan, Thady	91	Furlong, Nicholas	17, 107
Flanegan, Patrick	79, 82		
Flanigan, Timothy	8		
Flann, Richard	32		
Flannigan, James	58	G	
Flannigan, Pierce	58	Gaffney, Jane	12
Fleming, Thomas	30, 93,	Gaffney, John	53
	106	Gogarty, John	94
Flemming, Richard	49, 50	Galavan, Patrick	59
Flin, William	22	Galdanagh, Owen	75
Flinn, Edmond	57	Gallagher, Dudley	75
Flinn, John	57	Gallagher, Edmond	76
Flinn, Patrick	88	Gallagher, Fergal	76
Flinn, William	95	Gallagher, Hugh	75
Flood, Francis	8	Gallagher, James	25
Flood, James	12	Gallagher, John	74(2), 74
Flyn, William	86		79
Flynn, Dominick	24	Gallagher, Mary	75
Flynn, Patrick	9, 97,	Gallavan, Matthias	56
	98	Gallery, Morgan	48, 49
Flynn, Thady	79	Gallway, John	79, 80
Fogarty, Martin	60	Garalaght, Bart.	39
Fogarty, Terence	52	Gargan, Bryan	71
Foley, Darby	30	Garvey, Patrick	13
Foran, Mary	28	Garvey, William	79
Forave, Honora	83	Garvin, Daniel	23
Forragher, Patrick	81	Gawny, John	79, 81
Forragher, Thomas	81	Gaynor, James	81
Forrest, Michael	41	Genarty, James	35
Forrest, William	66	Geogarty, John	94
Forrester, George	10	Gibbon, Maurice	53
Forster, George	94	Gibbons, William	37
Fortune, Andrew	34	Gibson, Hugh	66
Foster, Isaac	34	Giles, Ed.	66
Fowley, Connor	57	Gill, Dennis	14
Fox, Daniel	11, 85,	Gill, Mary	33
	95	Gillespie, Mary	74(2)
Frain, John	27	Gilmartin, Dennis	79

Gilstrap, John	14		Griffith, Michael	54
Ginnahane, Ellenor	43		Griver, Peter	37
Giraghty, David	85		Grivey, John	104
Girraghty, David	95		Gronty, Patrick	88
Glavin, Bartholomew	16		Groudy, Patrick	97
Glasco, Margaret	16		Guily, Mary	45, 46
Glascoe, Hugh	9, 103		Guiraty, Daniel	11
Glassan, David	51			
Glisan, Catherine	57			
Glisan, James	57			
Godfrey, John	44, 45		H	
Gogarty, John	9		Hacket, Edmund	8
Golding, David	37		Hackett, John	58
Goodale, Thomas	28		Hackett, Michael	57
Goodman, Thomas	93		Hagall, Michael	93
Goodwin, Sarah	17		Hagan, Margaret	65
Goodwin, Thomas	29, 106		Hagarty, Daniel	41
Gordon, James	37, 104		Hagarty, Richard	39
Gorman, Honora	12		Halfpenny, Mary	15, 91
Gorman, Judith	12		Halfpin, John	77
Gorman, Mary	11, 95		Hall, John	37
Gorman, Penelope	16		Hallinan, Michael	60
Gormill, Roger	29, 105		Hallinan, Thomas	61
Gormly, Cornelius	73		Haly, David	58
Gould, Patrick	39		Haly, Honor	52
Gow, Anstace	50		Hamerton, William	57
Grace, Patrick	29, 32,		Hamill, Nicholas	23
	93, 106		Hamilton, Catherine	40
Grady, Patrick	57, 61		Hamilton, John	76
Graham, Andrew	8		Hammon, Edward	51
Graham, Edmund	9		Hananage, James	98
Graham, Edward	94		Hand, Laurence	105
Graham, Robert	71		Hand, Lawrence	28
Grandy, Patrick	28		Hand, Margaret	17, 107
Grany, Cornelius	42		Handy, Robert	14
Gray, Michael	36		Hanlan, Darby	86, 95
Gray, Thady	85, 91		Hanlan, Edward	58
Green, Thomas	57		Hanlon, Edmond	70
Greene, John	59		Hanly, Ann	15
Greeve, Peter	79		Hanly, Thady	38
Grey, Thady	11		Hannon, Darby	53
Griffin, Mary	56		Hanton, Darby	11
Griffin, William	79		Hanton, Peter	34

Hanvy, Patrick	69	Heydon, Mary	16
Haraghton, William	58	Heyland, Dennis	37
Harahane, Thomas	97	Heyland, Patrick	23
Harcan, Bridget	79, 80	Hickey, Christopher	15
Harcan, Rosanna	79	Hickey, Mary	48(2)
Hardin, David	26	Hickey, Owen	41
Harding, Robert	13	Hickie, Daniel	53
Harper, James	68	Hicks, Jane	48(2)
Harrick, John	37	Hicky, Christopher	91, 92
Harrington, Catherine	43	Higgins, Barnaby	12
Harrington, John	40	Higgins, Dennis	79, 81
Harrington, Mary	46, 47	Higgins, Patrick	51
Harrower, William	76	Higgins, Teigue	58
Hart, Robert	9	Hill, John	9, 91
Hart, Roger	32		92, 94
Harvey, Edward	63	Hill, William	25
Hasson, Jon	76	Hinagan, Catherine	78
Hauraham, Philip	40	Hoare, Bartholomew	88
Haverty, Elizabeth	18	Hoban, Edmond	33
Haydon, Mary	107	Hobbs, Mary	11, 85
Heany, Darby	12		95
Heany, Mary	15, 17	Hoey, Anne	30
Heas, Darby	58	Hoey, Thomas	94
Heas, John	58	Hogan, Bryan	32
Heas, Maurice	47(2)	Hogan, Dominic	80
Hease, John	56	Hogan, Dominick	18, 105
Healy, Margaret	48	Hogan, Michael	29, 58,
Healy, Thomas	17, 47		106
Heany, James	79	Hogan, Owen	52
Hehir, Charles	83	Hogan, Thomas	58
Helay, James	53	Hogan, William	17
Henaghan, Catherine	80	Hoghegan, Thady	78
Henderson, David	97	Hollaghan, Philip	58
Henderson, William	72	Holland, Michael	42
Hendrick, David	86	Hopper, Peter	16
Henessy, John	49, 50,	Horahan, Thomas	28
	51	Hore, Bartholomew	97
Hennelly, David	44	Hored, Margaret	92
Hennesy, Richard	41	Hosey, Patrick	32
Hern, Thomas	24	Hough, Teigue	58
Herns, John	57	Howard, John	10, 94
Hesseran, Thady	33	Howard, Mary	92
Hessernan, James	53	Howran, William	55

Keary, Loughlin	106	Kelly, Michael	22, 31
Keating, Henry	10, 87, 96	Kelly, Patrick	16, 24, 31
Keatings, Michael	37	Kelly, Peter	36
Keef, John	44	Kelly, Richard	13
Keefe, Elizabeth	43	Kelly, Thady	79
Keegan, Bryan	7	Kelly, Thomas	8
Keely, Sarah	13	Kelly, William	28, 66
Keenan, Dunkan	73	Kelly, Winnefred	46
Keenan, Henry	73	Kelly, Winnifred	46
Keenan, John	65	Kenim, Richard	106
Keenan, Mary	13	Kenney, Michael	81
Keenan, Michael	61	Kennedy, Catherine	13
Keery, Hugh	66	Kennedy, Daniel	59
Kegan, Thady	81	Kennedy, Darby	32
Keiffe, Judy	16	Kennedy, Edmund	35, 58
Keiffe, Margaret	16	Kennedy,Honorah	22
Keighry, Michael	78, 80	Kennedy, Patrick	78
Kent, William	44, 45	Kennedy, William	18, 58, 105
Kelly, Bartholomew	50		
Kelly, Bryan	37, 78, 80	Kennelly, Bridget	45
		Kennelly, Daniel	45
Kelly, Daniel	28	Kenny, Bryan	79
Kelly, Darby	29, 93, 106	Kenny, John	81
		Kenny, Michael	78
Kelly, David	59	Kenny, Patrick	33, 38, 80, 93, 107
Kelly, Dennis	37, 44, 78		
Kelly, Ellenor	13, 91	Kenny, William	35
Kelly, Francis	23	Kent, Michael	44
Kelly, George	34	Keoghoe, Daniel	35
Kelly, James	26, 37, 40, 63	Keon, Richard	16
		Kerewine, Andrew	107
Kelly, Jane	16	Kernes, James	13
Kelly, John	22, 46, 47, 49, 68, 78, 80, 93	Kerr, Patrick	66
		Kerr, Thomas	68
		Kerry, Thomas	32
		Kerwan, Richard	35
Kelly, Margaret	14	Kettles, Absalom	68
Kelly, Martha	14	Kewing, Andrew	93
Kelly, Mary	12, 13, 65	Killeghane, Daniel	56
		Killegott, Maurice	42
Kelly, Maurice	34	Kilkelly, Patrick	94

Meagher, William	58	Moore, John	95
Mealy, Bridget	86	Moore, Patrick	29, 105
Mealy, John	81	Moore, Peter	62
Mealy, Mary	13	Moran, Dennis	7
Mealy, Rose	15	Moran, Edward	7
Meane, Hugh	73	Moran, John	78, 80
Meany, Mary	48(2)	Moran, Joseph	31
Mears, Martin	83	Moran, Patrick	22, 27
Mechan, John	26	Moran, Thomas	22, 86
Medlicot, George	7		95
Meehan, Patrick	23	Morcarty, Robert	40
Meenagh, Owen	23	Moreton, Margaret	68
Melchan, Jane	13	Morgan, Ed.	66
Mercer, Elizabeth	65	Morgan, Mary	12
Mercy, Elizabeth	15	Morgan, Michael	15
Mercy, John	12	Morgan, William	24
Merrihy, John	40	Moriarty, Robert	41
Middleton, Margaret	50	Morissy, Mary	32
Mihin, Nicholas	28	Morres, Richard	27
Millone, Thomas	56	Morrin, Andrew	28
Mills, Andrew	73	Morris, Mary	12
Mills, Robert	73	Morris, Hugh	14
Mills, William	13	Morris, Michael	8
Minister, Mary	44, 45	Morrison, Francis	80
Mirachane, Bryan	79, 82	Mortimer, John	45
Mitchell, Mary	74	Muckleroy, Catherine	27
Mohan, Patrick	25	Mulcahy, Darby	59
Mohill, Ellenor	56	Mulcahy, Edmund	41
Molloy, Honor	37	Mulcahy, John	59
Molloy, Martin	78	Mulcahy, Michael	59
Molloy, Patrick	8	Mulcane, James	56
Monaghan, Bryan	79, 81, 82	Mulhollan, Patrick	77
		Mulholland, Owen	17
Monnelly, Edmond	79	Mulholland, Patrick	27
Mooney, Daniel	58	Mullally, thady	78
Mooney, Elizabeth	15	Mullan, Edward	14
Mooney, Mathew	23	Mullan, Patrick	14
Mooney, Mortagh	78	Mullan, Peter	18
Mooney, Murtogh	80	Mullan, Robert	72
Mooney, Patrick	75	Mullane, Dennis	42
Moor, John	10, 68, 85	Mulledy, Patrick	38
		Mullegan, John	98
Moore, James	9	Mullican, Daniel	81

McIllvenan, James	66	**N**	
McJohn, Teigue	57	Naghten, Laughlin	82
McKay, Patrick	87, 96	Nagle, Rose	46, 47
McKearnan, Dennis	68	Nange, Elizabeth	15
McKendrick Patrick	14	Nary, Patrick	37
McKenna, James	64	Naughton, Ellenor	37
McKeon, James	78	Naughton, John	79
McKewin, James	69	Naughton, Margaret	37
McLoughlin, Edmond	71	Neal, Daniel	103
McLoughlin, James	74	Neal, Francis	9, 94
McLoughlin, John	55, 77	Neal, Gordon	33
McMahon, Arthur	11	Neal, Henry	28
McMahon, Con.	63	Neal, James	27
McMahon, Daniel	74	Neal, John	11, 52
McMahon, Mary	63	Neal, Mary	53
McMahon, Michael	68	Neal, Thomas	53
McMahon, Patrick	23	Neal, William	16
McManus, Bart.	8	Neale, Honora	83
McManus, Charles	72	Needham, Thomas	38, 107
McManus, Thady	37	Neill, Joseph	67
McMelty, Francis	72	Neill, Mary	12
McMoroy, Teigue	81	Neilan, Luke	78, 80
McMullen, Arthur	85, 95	Neiraghane, Patrick	79
McNahoe, James	38	Nelan, Humphry	78
McNally, Honora	15, 98	Nesbit, John	64
McNamara, John	35, 83	Newall, Thomas	98
McNamara, Patrick	83	Newham, James	107
McNamee, Hugh	74	Newman, James	17, 93
McNeight, Robert	66	Newton, Ann	64
McNeill, Francis	72	Nichane, Joan	41
McNemara, Joan	104	Nonan, Patrick	38
McNeny, Philip	63	Noonan, Daniel	61
McPadden, Patrick	79	Noonane, Ally	56
McQuade, Bryan	63, 73	Norris, Catherine	18
McQuade, Henry	73	Norris, David	60
McQuade, Patrick	73	Norris, Maurice	60
McRoddin, Edmond	74	Norton, Joseph	8
McRory, Patrick	76	Norton, Mary	13
McSharry, Thomas	78, 80	Nowlan, Edmund	35
McSwine, Neal M	75	Nowlan, John	30
McWeeny, Bryan	78, 80	Nowlan, Margaret	35, 105
		Nowlan, Stephen	7
		Nowlan, Thomas	58

Smith, Mary	16	Sullivan, Mary	53
Smith, Owen	70	Sullivan, Thomas	14
Smith, Patrick	18, 105	Sullivan, Timothy	43, 45
Smith, Rose	75	Sumaghan, Thomas	78
Smith, Timothy	70	Sunnaghan, James	80
Smyth, George	23	Supple, Patrick	59
Smyth, Patrick	22	Sweeney, Roger	93, 107
Sowny, James	49	Sweeny, Catherine	48, 49
Spencer, Francis	78	Sweeny, Dennis	56
Spencer, Matthew	8	Sweeny, Mary	47
Spillane, Darby	57	Sweeny, Miles	46(2)
Spillane, Dennis	56	Sweeny, Morgan	57
Spillane, Maurice	42	Sweeny, Owen	55
Stack, James	55	Sweeny, Roger	8
Stack, John	56	Sweetman, Peter	8
Stack, Maurice	54	Swords, Richard	23
Stanley, George	45, 46	Synnott, Patrick	30
Staunton, Edward	16		
Staunton, Peter	64		
Steel, Adal	74		
Steel, Alexander	66	T	
Steel, James	64	Tallant, Thomas	85, 95
Stephens, Elizabeth	14	Tallent, Thomas	11
Stewart, George	77	Tallon, Andrew	24
Stewart, James	25	Tallon, Hugh	59
Stewart, William	33	Taylor, Ann	17
Stinson, George	75	Taylor, Thomas	69
St Leger, Anthony	78, 80	Tearnan, Thomas	94
Stone, Mary	93	Ternan, Matthew	10
Stoner, Mary	107	Terrill, Ann	65
Stones, Mary	17	Terrill, John	12
Street, John	39	Terrill, Richard	15
Stuokagh, William	58	Tholmey, Thomas	95
Sullivan, Catherine	43	Tobin, James	60
Sullivan, Charles	49, 50	Tobin, John	14
Sullivan, Darby	56, 61	Toole, Charles	30(2)
Sullivan, Daniel	41	Toole, Edmond	106
Sullivan, Dennis	56, 39	Toole, Edward	93
Sullivan, Ellenor	42	Tornbury, Margaret	8
Sullivan, John	45, 56, 39, 41	Totall, Ann	65
		Touhy, Matthias	83
Sullivan, Julian	44, 45	Towel, John	68
Sullivan, Margaret	41	Tracy, Francis	53

Trassy, Philip	58	Waters, Mary	13
Trawly, John	81	Watkins, Cornelius	12
Tresom, Alice	107	Watson, William	71
Tresso, Alice	16	Watterson, John	69
Twomey, James	45	Waugh, William	66
Tyrell, William	11	Welsh, Honor	48
Tyrrell, Michael	24	Welsh, Lewis	59
Tyrrell, Richard	8	Welsh, Richard	78
		Whealan, Daniel	17
		Wheelaghan, James	36
		Wheeler, Joan	45
U		Whelan, John	12, 61
Ulster, Alice	93	Whelan, Michael	60
Underwood, John	88, 97, 98	Whelan, William	8
		White, Bridget	18
		White, Henry	8
		White, Hugh	25
		White, Laurence	37
V		White, Thomas	78, 80
Vardin, John	26	Wholaghan, Daniel	94
Vaughan, John	44, 46	Wilkinson, Thomas	16
Venables, Ralph	11, 85, 91	Williams, James	16
		Williams, John	13
Vickers, Archibald	12	Williams, Nathaniel	41
		Williams, Philip	91
		Williams, Thomas	23
		Williams, William	66
W		Wilson, Edward	10, 94
Wade, Edmond	52	Wilson, Laurence	68
Wael, Catherine	92	Wilson, William	64, 78, 80
Wale, Catherine	107		
Wall, Catherine	11, 86, 95	Winsmore, Elizabeth	14
		Withers, Robert	12
Walsh, James	8(2), 9, 30, 91, 92, 94	Wolaghan, Daniel	86
		Wright, Joseph	65
		Wrot, Margaret	77
Walsh, John	17, 61		
Walsh, Mary	8	Y	
Walsh, Patrick	31	Young, James	64
Walsh, Richard	80	Young, John	69
Walsh, Thomas	39		
Ward, John	36	Z	
Warren, Andrew	12	Ze Williams	92